The Hidden Gifts
Within the Trauma of Sexual Abuse

The Hidden Gifts

Within the Trauma of Sexual Abuse

By Keira Poulsen

Freedom House Publishing Co.

Copyright ©2018 Keira Poulsen

All rights reserved.

No part of this publication may be reproduced, stored in a retrieval system, or transmitted in any form or by any means, electronic, mechanical, photocopying, recording, or otherwise, without written permission of the publisher.

Published in the United States by
Freedom House Publishing Co.

ISBN: 978-1-7323689-0-3

Interior art and cover art by: Marie Lee

Book cover design by: Katie Mullaly, Surrogate Press®

Interior design by: Katie Mullaly, Surrogate Press®

To my five beautiful children,

You are my inspiration. You are the light in my days,
and I love each one of you so much.

To Dan,

Thank you for holding me up when I couldn't walk.
Thank you for loving me, as I broke into a million pieces.
You were my rock, my friend, and your love
held me through this time.
I love you.

Table of Contents

Preface: For Everyone 1

Prologue: For Your Rebirth 3

Chapter 1: Broken Pavement 5

Chapter 2: Face the Pain or Die 16

Chapter 3: God Speaks to Us 30

Chapter 4: Surrender Fear Face Christ 43

Chapter 5: The Illusion of Protection 55

Chapter 5: Run. Stuff. Numb it. 66

Chapter 6: Protecting the Monster 75

Chapter 7: Ask and Receive 84

Chapter 8: Your Greatest Weapon 97

Chapter 9: How Abuse Looks Every Day 111

Chapter 10: Are There Really Hidden Gifts Inside This Hell? 133

Chapter 11: Wash Their Feet 142

Chapter 12: "Bring Me Your Suffering…" 163

Preview of the Next Book: Warriors of Light 177

Acknowledgments 184

About the Author 187

Index 188

Preface
For Everyone

I believe that God will speak to us.

He will speak to us regardless of who we are, what we've done, what religion we belong to, or what title we might carry in this life. God is "no respecter of persons," as Peter says in Acts 10:34; He shows no partiality, no prejudice, no favoritism toward anyone.

To me that means that God doesn't need you to be special or holy in order to speak to you. He knows you and will speak to you. To anyone who decides to seek Him out and ask, He will give. It doesn't matter if you're worthy or not. If you take the action to *seek*, He will answer and guide you.

Because of the fall of Adam and the veil that was put between us and God, we don't naturally just hear Him speak to us. Instead He finds ways to teach us and guide us. I believe He teaches us through whatever manner He can. A lot of times that way is through the verses and scriptures we read. So if you grew up reading the Bible, you most likely hear and receive from Him through those verses. Likewise, if you grow up reading the Quran, it's in those verses that you hear the voice of God.

As for me, I was raised on the verses in The Book of Mormon and in the Doctrine and Covenants. A lot of the answers I received from God were given to me though those verses and stories. These were the words that had been printed on my heart. I believe God used them to answer me, guide me, and at one time ultimately save my life.

As I began editing this book, I hit a wall. I considered taking out those verses because I didn't want people to think this book is only for Mormons.

Sexual abuse transcends all religions, races, gender, and countries. It's a dark plague that hits every community and every corner of this earth.

I wanted everyone to feel comfortable reading this book. But if I took out those few verses, I knew my story would not be fully authentic. Those verses and the insights held within them were the saving grace for me when I no longer wanted to live. I knew I couldn't take them out. If I'm sharing my true story with you, then it needs to be 100 percent authentic and accurate.

So I chose to leave them in.

I share this so you can hear and understand where I've come from and who I am.

The principles I was taught during my healing process are for all people—no matter your belief system or religion, and no matter your situation. Truthfully, these principles aren't only for those who've been sexually abused; they can guide anyone to find the gifts awaiting us on the other side of pain and trauma. But since my experience was with the trauma of sexual abuse, this is where I can lend the most help and insight.

Because of the shame, guilt, and loneliness that can suffocate victims of sexual abuse, I wanted to direct this book to them.

To *you*.

So that the lie that has permeated your life—saying, "You're alone"—will be shattered.

So that the truth of your worth and of the greatness that lies within you will be awakened.

I pray that this book will find peace and rest within your soul.

Prologue
For Your Rebirth

I believe there's a gift hidden within the trauma of sexual abuse.

What. The. Hell?

Yes. I can hear you.

I can hear the obscenities you must be yelling at me.

How dare I even write that sentence?

Clearly, I have no idea what trauma is or the insufferable pain that comes from sexual abuse.

I can hear you giving me details of your life as proof that I'm wrong. You can show me how the trauma and the deepness of pain has found its way into every crevice of your life. And the idea that there might be a gift in that hell makes you want to throw this book aside.

I know.

I also know that you may think I'm discrediting the pain you've been through.

But I'm not.

I know the insanity this pain has brought you.

I know the running you've done.

I know the shame, guilt, fear, and irate anger you've had to hide your whole life.

I know.

I know because I am you. I am a mirror of you who are. All of us who've been through this hell are alike.

You may feel like you're unlike anyone.

You most likely have felt this way ever since you were abused.

This is one of the darkest pieces of sexual abuse. You had to endure not only the sexual abuse, but also the lingering effect of feeling so alone. It is bitter and frighteningly real. This constant awareness that you're unlike others is always there, loud in your ears.

The constant hum that says you're totally different from anyone else is always there.

No one understands you.

No one thinks like you.

No one understands the fear that rules your daily life or the anxiety that creeps in like a burglar and strangles your breath.

Lies.

All lies.

Because... *we are all alike.*

Those of us who've endured this abuse are alike. And when I began to find others, and I realized this truth, there was a freedom that burst out of me. I knew I couldn't keep my mouth shut any longer.

This lie must be exposed.

This captivity that you feel must be broken. *This abuse will no longer win.*

And I promise you that there is a gift within this hell, a gift that will change your life.

It will be your rebirth.

I promise you also that this pain that's been dragging you through the mud, over sharp rocks and deep holes, can be gone.

Are you ready to walk with me? Are you ready to find the gift that's waiting for you?

Chapter One
Broken Pavement

When I was eighteen, I went to massage therapy school, where we were required to take a class on each modality of massage.

One of the many modalities was cranial sacral massage.

I remember the class well. This modality was unlike any of the others I'd learned so far. There's little physical touch involved in this form of body work. A lot of the work is done with light compression and energy work. The main intention of this modality is to help regulate the cerebrospinal fluid and clear any restrictions within the body.

The teacher taught us that it was common to have powerful dreams or insights when having the cranial sacral work done. I thought that was interesting, and I was hopeful. I was a young eighteen-year-old, filled with hope and faith.

I lay down on the massage table, as the client. The room was dark and quiet. The usual musty smell of massage lotions and oils permeated the dingy room. The school itself felt old and dirty, but I was used to the smells and the dinginess. I closed my eyes and tried to focus on the flow of energy and fluid through my spine and up into my cranium.

As I quieted my mind and allowed myself to relax, I felt myself fall asleep. Soon a vision or dream appeared in my mind.

I was five years old. I was covered all over in scrapes, cuts, and blood. I was sitting on the jagged pavement of the street outside my childhood home. The street was empty, and it was quiet all around me. I could feel the big tree behind me. I sensed no one else there. The houses were empty of people, and the streets were void of cars.

I remember sitting there with my shoulders slumped, crying deep cries. I felt a lot of pain and very alone.

Then a light appeared and seemed to surround me. When I looked up, Christ was standing there. He looked down at my broken five-year-old self. His gaze was one of pure love and acceptance. Acceptance of me, in my battered, bloodied, broken state. He picked me up in his arms and carried me down the street. As He held me, all of my wounds were healed. Peace came over me, and the loneliness left.

I woke up with tears streaming down my face. I didn't want to be there in that dark dingy room. I wanted to go back to that old street corner. I wanted to be back in the arms of my Savior. I wanted to feel that peace and love I'd felt for such a short moment of my life.

Then I began to question. Did I really have this dream-like experience, or did my mind just make up this vision? What did I actually experience in that dark, old, musty room? Had this vision been real? If so, why had I been given this gift?

I knew it was real. I knew, because I knew that little five-year-old girl. I knew her pain. I knew her brokenness. I knew that deep hurt and loneliness. Those cuts and scrapes were symbols of the pain I held inside my soul. I knew she needed to be healed. This vision was a gift for me, a gift of hope and healing.

You see, when I was a little five-year-old girl, I'd been sexually abused by my babysitter on a regular basis.

Every Friday night, my parents hired the same babysitter. They hired only one babysitter because my parents were very protective of us. They refused to have anyone else babysit us. This babysitter was their good friend's daughter and the safest babysitter they knew of, which was very important to my parents.

My family has had a long history of sexual abuse—those who came before me, and those who came before them. Because of this, I know how hard my mother tried to protect me from the vile beast that is sexual abuse. I know the energy she put forth to keep us safe. And from every outside evidence, this babysitter was the right choice.

The crappy part about sexual abuse is that the more you run from it, the faster it seems to find you.

And so it found *me*. In an unpredictable way. My abuser, who was the daughter of my parents' friend, and just a sweet kind girl from the neighborhood. And the abuse occurring in the safety of my very own home. I—the "victim"—kept quiet about the abuse I received. I didn't tell anyone due to fear, shame, and all the other horrible plagues tied to sexual abuse. I was afraid that she would get into trouble. I was deeply afraid that I would be in trouble as well.

So every Friday, for a long time, this abuse occurred.

Something I've noticed as I've worked with victims of abuse is that when someone is abused on a regular basis, they start to "shift out" emotionally and mentally. They do this so they don't have to be present when they're being abused. I'm guessing that this happened to me, since I don't have a lot of memories from the abuse. And for that, I'm grateful. I'm grateful I have only a few short memories from that time.

But I do know that I ran from that pain my whole life. It chased me like a howling wind, always screaming in my ears and always present. I was certain that if I ran fast enough or made life busy enough, then I wouldn't have to hear it or feel it. I was even more certain that if I lived my life perfect, then no one would ever know the darkness that seemed to be stuffed deep down. For that's what abuse feels like—a dark monster hidden in your soul, a darkness that can slow you down and eventually suffocate you. It's like an unforgiving molasses. It seeps into every part of who you are and into every crevice of your life. It taints the window that you view life from. It brings with it the heaviest of pain and the darkest of days.

I chose to run.

I chose to be perfect.

I really believed that if I lived my life so perfect, then no one would see the darkness that resided inside me. I hoped that if I was perfect enough, no one would view me differently.

I believed that by living more perfectly, I could erase the abuse that had left emotional scars within me. There was this insanity inside me saying that if I lived perfect and looked perfect, I'd feel better. Most of all, I hoped the pain would leave.

I believe that this is one way a victim of sexual abuse deals with their pain. There are many other ways victims cope and deal with their pain and their memories. This was my vice. The illusion of perfection lured me in with the pretense that told me that when I was perfect at whatever, I'd be happy, loved, accepted, good enough, worthy, etc.

But that never happened. Because once I reached a certain level of perfection in some area, then the next area would pop up. There was always a carrot being dangled in front of me, tempting me with the lies and illusions no matter how perfect I tried to be, I still felt the unhappiness, the feelings of being unaccepted, unloved, and not good enough.

Lies. Lies that are wounds from the abuse, lies that only pull us further down. When we finally catch that beautiful, delicious carrot on a stick we've been chasing, it turns out to be rotten and filled with worms.

The pain was always there, waiting for me to crash and burn. When I broke, my world pulled apart, leaving me in shambles. When I finally broke, all that I'd ever known to be true or right seemed to alter. I couldn't even remember what was true or what was false. When this pain began to finally consume me, I questioned all I'd ever known and all that my life had ever been.

For me, my abuse had just been brushed under the rug, and I'd never looked back. After I finally told my parents what had been happening on those Friday nights, I never spoke of the abuse to them again. I'm sure in all their many prayers and longings they hoped that the abuse would have no lasting effect on me. I'm sure they hoped I would heal. They were wonderful parents and did the best they could. But like any parents of a child who's abused, they had to deal with their own grief and pain over this. No parent is equipped to deal with the truth that their five-year-old daughter has been abused by a babysitter they had trusted while they were gone.

As much as they hoped that I would move on and heal from the abuse, that's not how it went for me. Instead I began to view the world through the glasses of abuse. Everywhere I went, I viewed everyone I met through those glasses. I would ask myself, "Is this person safe? Will this person hurt me? Is this a safe place, and if not, how do I get out?" These questions and many more filled my mind as a little child. Each situation, each person had to be measured on my inner abuse ruler. This, for me, was a full-time job.

I also found myself always worried for everyone around me. I would feel compelled to watch over everyone I was with. This carried through to all my relationships and interactions. The fear that someone I loved was being abused was a constant worry in my mind. I was always checking out all the situations I was in and making sure everyone was safe. If one of my siblings was in a room with a friend, I'd have an intense panic attack. I'd fling open the door and burst in, always afraid I'd find them in an abusive situation like I had experienced.

The abuse glasses.

They were always there. I could never take them off.

This was my inner dialogue as a child, and I never shared these thoughts with anyone. I kept it all nice and tightly wound within me. I continued to follow all the rules and continued to be as perfect as I possibly could be. The more perfect I tried to be, the tighter I grew inside.

This resulted in my being a quiet and introverted child. I was shy, and I found my joy in things like reading or baking chocolate chip cookies with a cousin on the weekends. I had my "safe people," and this continued throughout my life, even into adulthood. The experience of having only a few friends to hold close and keep each other safe is one I've always known.

As with most people who have deep pain, I was drawn to an art. For me, it was the art of dance. This was my one place of freedom. In the freedom of dance I could set free all my pain. It was my gift. The talent God gave me was His saving grace for me.

Dance was my outlet for pain. When I began to dance, I found that I was able to live life more fully. I became extroverted. I loved having friends and laughing. I was a joyful, carefree teenager. I believe this was because when I danced, I didn't run from my pain anymore.

To be more precise, it was while I danced that I allowed myself to feel and bear the pain in a different way, and the pain in my normal life would dim and get less.

There's a powerful lesson in this, one I wouldn't fully understand until twenty years later. The lesson is this: *When we finally decide to feel the pain we've hidden, freedom occurs, and joy begins to flow.*

There's a healing agent in feeling the pain. It's like the sting often associated with cleansing a wound on the body, a cleansing that must occur before the wound can heal. It's the same with our inner selves. We must deal with our pain so we can fully heal.

Aristotle said that we cannot learn without pain. This is a mantra I've come to live by. There's freedom when we understand it. It's one of the first things we discover in the story of Adam and Eve. Eve knew that for her and Adam to grow and to learn, they had to pass through the pain and the trials of this world. In her divine feminine wisdom, she knew that this was the only way. This is one of the founding truths in the scriptures. No matter what book you're in or what prophet's words you read, trials and pain are the pathway of growth.

Residing in most of our lives and cultures is a lie that says you shouldn't have pain. This is one of the many reasons why so many people's lives are governed by addictions to numb the pain they want to escape. Many of us feel like we're doing something wrong if we have pain. Or we believe that if we want to be happy, we can't have pain. But I believe it's through the pain that we find our happiness and become the person we were created to become.

One of my favorite quotes is this line from the Persian poet Rumi: "The wound is where the light enters you."

So it is with us.

Therefore I'd like to call us "the gifted ones."

Those of us who've felt a pain that no one else has felt are the gifted ones. We've felt the pain of what happened to our bodies. The pain of feeling abandoned by those who were put in charge of protecting us. The pain of immense fear and self-doubt that follow this type of abuse so stubbornly and continually. And then of course the deep pain of loneliness and disconnectedness that now form the background of all our relationships.

But with all this pain, we're gifted with a chance to fully heal. Because of these wounds, we allow greater access for light to enter into us. In this healing we become greater than we ever could have without the pain. It's that rebirth of who we are that illuminates our path with light and freedom.

The pain is the bridge to our healing.

The pain is one of the hidden gifts.

Not only does our personal pain break us open and allow light to enter and heal us; but *we* can be that light for those around us. We're gifted with a deep awareness of self and of others. We naturally have an empathy for those in pain. Because we know pain, we can feel and sense another's pain more quickly and acutely than most people can.

More than likely, you haven't thought of this as a "gift." I know it can seem unbearable to feel other people's pain so instinctively. But when you begin to see this as one of your gifts, you'll be able to see how you can be a light for those who are drowning in a depth of pain that only a few know and understand. You are one of those few.

As the poet Rumi says, "The cure for the pain is the pain."

Chapter One Journaling

When and where did your abuse occur? What do you remember from this time of your life? What are the thoughts that you have around this abuse?

_____

_____

_____

_____

_____

_____

_____

_____

_____

_____

_____

_____

_____

_____

_____

_____

_____

_____

_____

_____

_____

Broken Pavement

The Hidden Gifts

What pain are you hiding? What pain are you numbing up, running from, and ignoring? How do you manage the pain when it shows up in your life?

_____

_____

_____

_____

_____

_____

_____

_____

_____

_____

_____

_____

_____

_____

_____

_____

_____

_____

_____

_____

_____

What would life look like if you didn't have to run, hide or numb your pain? Who would you be if you could break free from this pain?

_____
_____
_____
_____
_____
_____
_____
_____
_____
_____
_____
_____
_____
_____
_____
_____
_____
_____
_____
_____
_____
_____

Chapter Two
Face the Pain or Die

"There is no such thing," writes Richard Bach, "as a problem without a gift for you in its hands." My brain couldn't understand this line when I first read it in the novel *Illusions*. But I felt my spirit scream at me that this quote was important. I tucked it into my brain until the day came when it all unfolded before me.

It's the day I realized there was actually a gift hidden within this problem. That there was a gift, if I chose to look face-first at my abuse. No more blinders, no more disguises, no more shields. And most of all:

No. More. Running.

It was face it, or die.

Plain and simple.

Since I was fourteen, I've struggled with suicidal thoughts. No actions were ever taken, but the thoughts would come. And they would get loud. Louder and louder, until the force of them would almost knock me over.

Dancing would take the edge off my pain when I was a teenager. But the older I got, the more stress I felt. The loneliness grew and seemed to suffocate me. Because I chose to be as perfect as I possibly could to hide my abuse, I never let anyone know about these thoughts. I was a happy, joyful teenager and adult; if you were to meet me, you would never have guessed that suicide was on my radar. I was good at hiding my pain. I was excellent at trying to ignore what was screaming deep down inside me.

But those thoughts were still there. They came when life started to get hard. They came when loneliness showed up, or when I felt hurt emotionally. Every single confrontation, every moment of being upset, would feel like the end of the world for me.

It was like there was a vault inside my soul where all the pain of the abuse was stored, and every time I would get hurt or upset, the door to this vault would blast open. Instead of experiencing a normal level of pain or discomfort from a particularly stressful circumstance, I instead encountered waves of overwhelming pain.

This is what happens when we run from our abuse pain. Little moments in life that are hard or painful can take us down the darkest and deepest rabbit holes. It takes us there because it taps into the pain we haven't dealt with. This is why I believe so many victims of sexual abuse deal with suicidal thoughts. The pain is so great and so heavy and shows up way too often. To live a life filled with that much pain is mostly unbearable.

It was during these moments when the suicidal thoughts would come. These thoughts of suicide were detailed, and I saw images in my head of how to move forward with each plan. I hated this. I felt cursed. Why couldn't I just be like everyone else and worry about normal everyday worries? Instead I had to try and clear my brain of the step-by-step instructions my demons were making for me.

Until one day I learned: *that was exactly what they were—demons.*

I'd started to learn how to facilitate a type of emotional healing work called muscle testing. I'd been attending school for it, and I loved it. Stepping into the role of a facilitator allowed me to discover a lot of the spiritual gifts I had. One of those gifts happened to be the ability to see beyond this physical world. I wouldn't have described this as a gift back then, but it turned out to be one of the greatest gifts of my life.

I started seeing images of dark spirits around people I was helping. These spirits were accompanying the pain of the clients I was working on. I saw that each spirit looked different, and they were never light.

Soon, I saw these types of spirits frequently. It was a dark time in my life: I was a mother of four small children, living a busy and full life, yet I was also having to see beyond this world into what I can only describe as complete hell.

But even in that hell, there was a beautiful gift for me: the realization that thoughts of suicide were *not* coming from myself, but were being pushed into my mind by dark spirits. These demons were feeding me the step-by-step instructions on how to kill myself, giving me reasons for why I should leave this world. They were the pushers.

Knowing this was the piece that freed me. I was freed from thinking I was crazy. I finally saw that I wasn't a horrible person for having these thoughts. The guilt, shame, and pain that I'd always felt for having these thoughts left me.

And then I had power over my suicide.

I learned that all I had to do was to ask Christ to come and take these spirits away from me. As soon as I prayed for that, the suicidal thoughts would be gone.

Completely gone.

There's no right way to ask Christ to come and help you. You will know. You don't need to be part of a certain religion or have a certain faith. You just have to believe. And then you must ask. Open your mind and heart and allow yourself to be taught how it is that *you* ask Christ to help you with these thoughts and this problem.

I believe that Christ would save us from all our pain. But I'm also a believer that we were given the law of agency, and Christ abides the boundaries of that law. This means that He can't come and save us *unless we invite Him or ask Him to.*

I started to feel an enormous difference. When the first thought of suicide would show up, I would say a quick prayer that went like this:

My dear Father, I ask that Christ will come into this room and gather in all the darkness and spirits who are pushing these thoughts into my mind [and here I would name each thought as it had come]. I ask that Christ would place this darkness in a sphere of light and take them to wherever Christ would have them go. And please, Father, pour Christ's light over me and this room to cleanse me from any darkness that's left over. And please allow the light of Christ to heal me and make me whole.

In the name of Jesus Christ,

Amen.

This became a routine prayer for me. And I found that I had power over these horrible thoughts. I was freed from this debilitating sickness of suicidal thoughts. I began to understand what it felt like to work hand in hand with asking and receiving from Christ.

I used to believe that I had to be worthy or special or really spiritual to know Christ. But when I started to ask Him for His divine help, I was amazed that *every* time I asked these requests in prayer, these horrible thoughts would leave.

Every time.

I didn't see Christ. I didn't touch Him or even hear Him. But I knew He showed up for me when I asked, and I knew that He would always help me.

I learned how powerful it is just to ask.

I learned deeply that light always overcomes darkness.

I learned how powerful the light of Christ is. And that when we seek Christ and His light, *all is possible.*

During that period of my life when I saw spirits, life was dark. I would find myself asking Christ to sit next to my bed at night to keep the darkness away. I hated the darkness I saw. I feared the darkness. But the more I feared, the more dark spirits would show up. I began to see that fear was their front-row ticket into my life. *Fear is what gave them access to me.*

I know how huge fear is in the life of a victim of sexual abuse. There's the fear of the abuse happening again. Fear of others finding out that you've been sexually abused. Fear of those you love being abused.

Fear.

Fear.

And more fear.

I lived my life out of fear. No wonder I had so much darkness surrounding me. As I learned how to ask for the darkness to be taken away, fear started to leave, since fear and faith cannot reside within the same space. I began to see how fear had been canceling out any faith I had. Fear was like quicksand for me. One step in, and I would be paralyzed with the level of fear that hit me. But as soon as I let go of fear, faith would grow stronger. Faith in a God and a Savior who knew me and loved me. Faith that I would live and be happy. These started to fill my mind and my heart instead of the fear that had taken root for too many of my years.

I know this is a lot to take in for you as a reader. If you've never thought like this, it must be hard to comprehend. But I know that if you've been burdened with suicidal thoughts, you're also willing to try anything. I know the heaviness this burden causes. I know the shame and guilt you feel for having these thoughts. And I know that you think you're alone.

But the more I've talked with other people who've been sexually abused, the more I've learned that they all have suicidal tendencies. Most suffer from heavy depression and anxiety. Each woman who has spoken to me has told me of her fight to live. Each one has told me the burden it has been to fight those suicidal thoughts. To fight the thoughts is heavy enough, but then just as heavy are the shame and the guilt for having those thoughts. This has been a consistent thread I've found in common with every other abused victim. You may be one of the lucky ones, and this may never have been your burden. But if it has been your burden, I want you to know you're not alone. And even more, I hope you believe me when I tell you, that these thoughts are *not* your thoughts. That you're *not* the one who sits and plans out your death. And more importantly, that you have access and freedom from these thoughts. It will take work, and it will seem unbelievable at first.

But it will be worth it.

You'll have freedom and control over your thoughts regarding suicide. It will free your mind to do the great things you were meant to do.

Another common thread I found was that each woman I met who'd been sexually abused had a bright light within them. I was always drawn to them. I felt like I knew them. Their light was like mine. I've always had this light within me. I've had a joy that has seemed to pull me through the darkness and fear that has been the crust of my life. And these women had the same light and joy.

It gave me only one conclusion: We are so much the same!

And how ugly it is that abuse isolates us and lies to us by filling our minds with thoughts that say, "I am alone. No one's like me. No one can ever understand me."

How false that is! When I began to discover I wasn't alone in my suicidal thoughts and my fears and anxieties, I felt a massive relief. I felt like I'd just figured out a math equation that had seemed impossible before.

These things that I hated about myself were the results of the abuse that happened to me. And for some reason, knowing that freed me. It freed me from my isolation. It freed me from the guilt that had been weighing me down. It freed me from the belief that I was the reason for all these problems. Instead, these problems I was dealing with were part of the abuse I'd been through.

These are the effects of abuse. Just like having chicken pox makes you itchy and red, being a victim of sexual abuse has the effect of bombarding you with suicidal thoughts, depression, and anxiety.

Knowing this gave me the choice to heal. It also pushed me to write this book. What if I could reach others who felt as I did and help free them from their isolation and darkness? I knew I couldn't keep my mouth shut. I knew that what I'd learned must be shared.

The Hidden Gifts

There are too many of us walking around, clouded by the noise in our heads and the burdens on our shoulders. We zip it all up, stuff it down deep, and use the inner strength we've been blessed with to move through life as gracefully as possible. There's a level of exhaustion that comes from keeping it all together. But the fear that it might all just tumble out of us one day pushes us to keep walking, keep running, and never stop.

Until the day comes when we cannot run anymore.

Then it's time to finally deal with the pain.

Chapter Two Journaling

Have you ever suffered from suicidal thoughts? If so, what do you say to yourself around them? Do you make yourself wrong and bad for having these thoughts?

_____

_____

_____

_____

_____

_____

_____

_____

_____

_____

_____

_____

_____

_____

_____

_____

_____

_____

_____

_____

Allow yourself to see that you are not the cause for these suicidal thoughts. How does that sentence make you feel? How does it feel to understand that you are not the source of those dark thoughts and plans?

_____

_____

_____

_____

_____

_____

_____

_____

_____

_____

_____

_____

_____

_____

_____

_____

_____

_____

_____

Face the Pain or Die

I want you to write out your worth and greatness. What are the parts of you that are GREAT?! Be kind to yourself as you write these out; there is no need to be modest. This is only for you!

_____
_____
_____
_____
_____
_____
_____
_____
_____
_____
_____
_____
_____
_____
_____
_____
_____
_____
_____
_____

I want you to write out the fears, the shame and the guilt you have been carrying around from your abuse. What do they look and feel like in your everyday life?

Do you think that you have the courage to ask Christ to help take these thoughts away? What are the thoughts that are running in your mind around this idea? What stops you from asking Him?

What would life look like if you could really allow Christ to take this burden for you? How would life be if you had power over suicidal thoughts?

_____

_____

_____

_____

_____

_____

_____

_____

_____

_____

_____

_____

_____

_____

_____

_____

_____

_____

Write here three times "I choose to live!"

_____

_____

_____

Chapter Three
God Speaks to Us

God knows us. He not only knows us, but He knows who we are. He knows the possibility and greatness that we're to become. And by our knowing Him and seeking Him, we get access to that knowledge. We get to see ourselves through His looking glass instead of the corrupted, tainted lens that we tend to see ourselves through.

I know that when I've talked openly with others about God and how He answers our prayers, the most common response I've received is, "God doesn't speak to me"—which I believe isn't true. Often we don't know *how* He speaks to us.

I believe He speaks to each one of us differently. But because we don't know how God speaks individually to us, we don't hear Him when He speaks.

I came to realize that asking for God's help in this is something that needs to become part of our prayers. Not only asking God for an answer, but asking Him to teach us how to hear Him. How does He speak to us individually? If that piece is shown to us, how different would life be! What would life be like for you if you were able to speak with God and receive from Him on a personal level?

I'm certain that life would be very different for you.

I believe all this is possible. Not only do I believe it, but I hope for this. Because if this isn't possible, life has a bleak and dismal existence for me. I believe there's more to this life than just surviving, more than just existing. I don't believe God sent us here to just survive and exist. I believe He has work for us to do. And for that to be accomplished, we have to be able to hear Him. We have to connect with Him and allow Him to lead us hand in hand through this life.

But for many of us who've been through sexual abuse, we wonder where God was during that abuse. Or maybe you don't believe God knows you. Maybe you don't believe in God at all. I'm sure we've all wondered at times: *How could God have let me go through the trauma I went through? Where was He? He must not be a God of mercy or love. Why?*

You most likely have sat in your ocean of pain and yelled out, asking how God could have left you in your time of need.

I believe these thoughts are normal. Not only are they normal, but they're part of the process of healing from abuse. These thoughts are what breaks down all our belief systems.

I've wondered all these questions and many more throughout my days of darkness and pain.

I distinctly remember the day when I thought God had completely forgotten me and left me alone in this world. It was this exact moment that broke me down to nothing. It was this moment that changed my life forever. The moment where I had to feel all my abuse pain for the first time in my life. It was when the gates of hell seemed to break loose, and I didn't know if I would last one more day.

I thought that I'd dealt with the trauma of my abuse. It didn't haunt my conscious thoughts in any way. I felt like I'd forgiven my abuser and that everything about that was in the past for me. I was thirty-four years old; the abuse had occurred when I was five, so the trauma felt like lifetimes ago. And I was certain I'd healed from that trauma.

I've always seen myself as a strong individual. I've been through a number of other difficult trials, and I've faced them with a force of strength and strong will. Most things don't make me crack. I've always been able to see a silver lining within the hardships and have always tried to find God's hand in the hardest of times.

But nothing could have prepared me for the hell that was going to pour down upon me—and especially the weakness that ultimately would show up for me.

It was in the month of February, that my life changed for forever. A dear loved one came to me to share about having been violated sexually by someone. The event could be considered minor in the realm of abuse, though I'm not sure that's even relevant; *any* sexual violation is harmful and has long-lasting effects.

It was this moment that split open the cement walls I'd built around my own trauma. It was in this event that the pain I'd been holding deep down—stuffed there with the doors tightly shut—came rushing out.

I find it amazing that for twenty-nine years, I was able to essentially ignore the trauma that had happened to me. At some level I felt like I could handle it. I thought that I was stronger than most, and I supposed that this is why the abuse had happened to me. But when I felt the pain of any sort of abuse happening to someone else—someone I loved—I couldn't bear it.

It took a few days for me to be able to fully comprehend the pain that was showing up. At first, I was struck with denial and shock.

It felt like the first moment after bone is broken, that moment when the pain hasn't hit and the shock is in full force. Yet you sit there holding your arm, fully aware that it's broken, but unable to feel the awful pain that will hit at full force within an hour.

This was my experience with finally dealing with the trauma that had occurred for me as a child. The pain that I'd held off for twenty-nine years was just about to unleash upon me. And the only way I would ever have finally dealt with this pain was by experiencing the reality of someone I loved having to go through a similar trauma.

It was a day I still remember as if it was today.

It was a Thursday. My son was napping, my older kids were at school. It was one of the few minutes of the day when I was alone. I sat there on the floor of my office. I was on the phone with a sexual abuse hotline. I thought I was calling to receive information for my loved one, but instead I found myself dry-heaving through sobs as I spoke with a complete stranger. I remember her telling me that she thought it sounded like I might need to get help. She seemed very concerned for me. She explained that this experience was most likely bringing up the pain and trauma from when I had been abused as a child.

When I hung up the phone, I was so angry. Wasn't she hearing me? *I* didn't need help! My loved one needed help. *I* was fine! *I* had healed! I wasn't the one with the problems anymore.

Then the tidal wave hit.

It hit me like a thousand bricks and I could no longer breathe.

On a scale of one to ten, the pain I felt was at least fifty. I didn't know such consuming pain was even possible.

So much anger. So much hurt. So much pain pumped through my veins.

But out of all the reasons to be angry about, and all the people to be angry with, I was most angry with one.

And that was God.

I've always felt a close relationship with God. In all my hours of praying through my life, I'd made it quite clear to Him that He owed me one thing. And that one thing was to keep those I loved safe from anything connected to the experience of sexual abuse. I had more faith in this than in anything else. I believed that God owed me that.

He had not protected me from the abuse I went through, but I still loved Him and worshiped Him; therefore the least He could do for me was to always protect those I loved. How hard would this be? I knew He could do this. And I always believed He would.

How could God now let me down? Where was He? Didn't He remember our agreement?

This all seemed logical to me. The God I believed in could part the Red Sea and heal the dying. This was the God I worshiped. So how in the hell did He break this promise with me?

I was so angry with Him. I felt like He had fully betrayed my trust, and I lost all faith in Him. In that moment, I lost all faith in this experience of life.

Everything I'd learned about suicide and being able to clear the room and myself of those dark spirits left me. The years of learning how to have control over suicidal thoughts were useless in that moment.

I willingly surrendered to all the thoughts, all the fears, and all the pain.

I was done.

I was done living in a world filled with so much pain, so much fear, so much hurt. I was done living in a world where the God I believed in and the God who I thought loved me so much had left me alone.

Why would I keep fighting for my life over and over if this one God—who I'd trusted to love me, speak to me, and guide me—didn't hold up His side of our bargain?

I was done.

I decided I wouldn't stop the voices of suicide that day. Today would be the day when all this pain would finally end.

As I lay on the ground, sobbing and exhausted, something deep down inside me reached over for my phone and called my neighbor.

The phone rang. It rang and it rang. No answer.

"This is it," I thought.

I hated God even more now. Couldn't God even get my neighbor to answer her phone to help save me?

It was apparent to me now that He'd really left me alone. How could He let me do this?

He was gone. I couldn't feel God anywhere.

Then my phone rang and it was my neighbor. A tiny sliver of light returned.

In God's grace, He had brought this old friend of mine to also be my neighbor. Earlier, she and I had attended school for muscle testing together, and she was aware of my past history of abuse from our time together in that class. It was because of our history together that allowed me to call her for help that day. I'm certain that on that day, I wouldn't have been able to call anyone else.

Only God could have orchestrated that situation.

He had *not* left me alone in this hell.

I'm extremely private about my life; I'd never shared with anyone the level of darkness or pain I've been through. But when she phoned me, and I told her I was about to commit suicide and that I needed her help, she quickly came over and let me lie on the ground sobbing and telling her that God had left me. I screamed that He had forgotten me and my one request of him.

She just sat and listened.

And I lived.

An hour later, it was time to go pick up my daughter from school.

One thing that abuse had taught me was that you just have to keep going, no matter what. This is a trait I'd carried though my whole life. And it proved to still be strong for me. I couldn't even imagine calling my daughter's teacher and telling her I was struggling so badly. I wasn't going to let anyone know my deepest secrets. And so I wiped my eyes and got in the car.

As I was driving over there, God's voice returned in my mind and I could see an image in my head. The image is one of Joseph Smith when he was in Liberty Jail. Let me paint the picture as I saw him in this jail. The jail was small, dark, and dirty. I saw Joseph sitting there in that dark, musty jail, and I saw him look up to the heavens. As he looked upward, I heard him say these words:

"O God, where art Thou? And where is the pavilion that covereth Thy hiding place? How long shall Thy hand be stayed, and Thine eye, yea Thy pure eye, behold from the eternal heavens the wrongs of Thy people and of Thy servants, and Thine ear be penetrated with their cries?"

I didn't know these verses. I'd read them a few times in my life. But God shared these verses with me because He knew that when I heard them I would realize I wasn't alone. I wasn't the first nor the last to ever feel as if God had forgotten them.

As I heard these words roll through my mind, I felt Joseph's pain. His pain was the same as mine. Here he was, sitting in a dark jail, sick, tired, and cold, and crying out to God the same words I'd been screaming: *God! Where are you?*

In the next verses, God responds:

"My son, peace be unto thy soul; thine adversity and thine afflictions shall be but a small moment; and then, if thou endure it well, God shall exalt thee on high; thou shalt triumph over all thy foes."

As I heard those words go through my mind, I knew that *if* I believed this, all this hell would be for my good.

A tiny seed of hope had been planted into my heart, the heart that had given up on hope. This heart that was barren and bleak now had a spark of light. This seed of hope would change the course of my life.

I soon arrived at my daughter's preschool. It was held at my friend's house, who lives on an acre. She has at least eight goats, twenty chickens, and a handful of bunnies on her acre.

I heard this thought come to my mind to go into her backyard. I figured this was because animals have always been healing for me, and if there was any time that I needed to feel healing, it was today.

Then the most miraculous event of my life showed up.

I walked into their backyard feeling broken, exhausted, and similar to a walking zombie. I felt dumb being back there. I'm sure I looked a little strung out from my hours of sobbing. I was still wearing my pajamas and I had the words *Surrender Fear* and *Face Christ* written in permanent marker all over my wrists (this had been one of my efforts to keep myself alive).

After being there for a few minutes and feeling embarrassed about how I looked, I decided to leave. As I was leaving, my friend started to scream. I looked over and one of her goats was giving birth. My friend cried that this wasn't supposed to happen; the goat wasn't due for another week, and had shown no signs of labor that day. But here it was, giving birth to a tiny baby goat. She yelled to me to get the supplies she needed for the birth. I quickly ran into her home to gather the bag of birthing supplies. I ran out forgetting all that happened earlier that day. I watched in amazement as the baby goat was being born. And in my mind, I could hear God whisper: "This is for you. This is a symbol of your rebirth. Allow all this pain to bring forth your renewal."

Tears were streaming down my face as I realize that God hadn't forgotten me. And what if all this shit, all the pain I'd been through, was for a bigger purpose? What if God was just allowing me to walk through this moment of hell to bring about a greater peace to my life?

After those wild moments of our excitement and anxious activity, the mother goat finally pushed out her kid into this world. But it was quickly apparent to both my friend and I that this baby goat was dead. My heart sank. How could this sweet goat die when I'd just felt God there with me? But my friend grabbed a towel and started rubbing and talking to this tiny goat. Before I knew it, the goat was moving! She was breathing! She would live!

As I sat there shaking from all that had just taken place, I looked at the tiny frail body covered in blood, and I knew that all this was for me. God had given me all this. This was proof to me that He hadn't forgotten me. And as this goat would live, I would live. I would thrive.

I decided right then and there that I would allow this hell to be my rebirth, whatever that might mean, however it might look.

Chapter Three Journaling

Do you believe God speaks to people?

_____

Do you believe He speaks to you?

_____

If you answered no, why do you believe He won't speak to you?

If you answered yes, how do you hear God? What are some ways and feelings you experience when He speaks to you.

_____

_____

_____

_____

_____

_____

_____

_____

_____

_____

_____

_____

_____

_____

God Speaks to Us

What does it mean to you if God speaks to you? What would life look like if you could hear God every day?

_____

_____

_____

_____

_____

_____

_____

_____

_____

_____

_____

_____

_____

_____

_____

_____

_____

_____

_____

_____

_____

I want you to start to listen for God. Ask Him HOW you will hear Him. And then start to listen.

Begin by asking God to open your ears, your heart and your mind to receive from Him. Even if you have never prayed before, step into this experiment with me. Ask Him to start to show you how to hear Him and how to receive.

Then take a few minutes every day to journal what you start to hear and feel in these next two pages:

**Today I began to ask God to speak to me.
Here is what I experienced today:**

_____

_____

_____

_____

_____

_____

_____

_____

_____

_____

_____

_____

_____

_____

God Speaks to Us

Chapter Four
Surrender Fear Face Christ

As I walked through my own healing path, I found that God had distinct principles for me to learn. (I'll be sharing these principles with you in the next few chapters.)

Each principle showed up along with new struggle and pain.

Though I'd experienced the miracle of the goat's birth, and I'd heard God say that my experience that day was to be *my* rebirth, it didn't mean that life got easier. Life actually got harder. For the first time in my life, I was letting myself feel the pain. I was no longer pushing it down, no longer running. I was facing it. Head-on.

As I did this, I crumbled, I shattered, and I no longer could hold up the appearance that I was perfect. For the first time in my life, I was broken. There were many nights where I would be in bed, sobbing, unable to move. My husband would wipe the snot off my face, lift me out of bed, and put me in the car. He would drive me to my favorite restaurant and get take-out food just so I would get out of the house.

Since I was five years old, I'd never allowed myself to feel any of the pain that had come from the abuse. It's like I hit the ground running and I never looked back. But this time I'd cracked, and the vault that had been hiding my pain had exploded. I felt like I was living life through a haze. I wasn't really present, but all my feelings and emotions were set on high.

The crying spells turned into a schizophrenia phase, or so I chose to call it. I began to think that everyone was a molester, and that those I loved would never be safe. I would wake up in the middle of the night in cold sweats, filled with panic. Panic that everyone in my life would hurt the people I loved most.

Everywhere I turned, everywhere I went, the fear that every person around me was a molester was blasted through my head. I started to feel insane. I wanted to lock my house, homeschool my kids, and teach church in my living room. I wanted to shut us out from everything and everyone.

I remember clearly the day I was driving down the freeway with all my children. The anxiety had just hit hard, and I started sobbing uncontrollably. I called Dan and told him to find the nearest mental institute. I needed him to check me in. I was officially going insane. I felt the craziness in my head hit an all-time high, and I knew I wasn't going to be able to raise five kids anymore, not like this.

Dan got home and helped talk me through my anxiety. His patience during this time, with his world turning upside down, was my greatest blessing. He never thought I was crazy, and he always talked me through my deepest struggles. But we both decided I needed help. I needed to find someone who could help me heal, and ultimately help me live.

So I prayed. I asked God to show me a therapist's name. Out of all the people in the therapy profession, I needed the one who was going to help me heal. It was my time to heal after hiding this pain for twenty-nine years.

That same day a friend of mine posted a request on Facebook, asking for referrals to a therapist. I saw names that friends were listing in their responses. Then one name stood out to me: Glenda Horning. I knew this was who God was sending me to.

At my first appointment with Glenda, I was scared to death. I'm not quite sure why. I think I was excited to finally be getting help but also scared to see what I'd been hiding from all these years. I was terrified to see what had been lurking in the back of my mind. I was so frightened to actually deal with the one thing I'd been running from for so long.

I walked into her room and Glenda was the most lovely woman, filled with so much light. She continued to walk me through all my levels of pain. She primarily used the method called Rapid Eye Technology, and this method started to work miracles for me. I began to see her once a week for a long time. Most days when I would leave her office, I would feel like someone had peeled layers off my skin. The level of pain and the feeling of being exposed was intense. But the results were miraculous.

Little seeds of miracles started to show up. One seed was the powerful feeling of being a warrior. I'd faced my greatest fear, and I'd lived. I hadn't died! And that feeling—that I'd defeated death and conquered my most frightening fear—left me with a deep power. Somedays I would wear my hair in warrior buns as I went out to Home Depot or Walmart; the words *Warrior of Light* were written on my wrists in permanent marker.

I was strong! Stronger than I ever knew! I continued to have Dan write on my wrists every morning my motto: *Surrender Fear. Face Christ.*

This was my daily mantra. So that every time I washed my hands or picked up my toddler, I was reminded that I was a warrior of light, and that I would surrender all my fear and face Christ. But most importantly, when those suicide thoughts would come, I would see my wrists, and these words gave me strength to be bold and brave. These words awakened my spirit and reminded me that Christ is always stronger than Satan.

Surrender Fear. Face Christ. These words were my saving grace.

This leads us to the first principle I learned in this time, that of **surrendering fear**. What does that look like? How does one do that?

For me, I'm very visual. So I close my eyes and I imagine an altar. This altar is just for me, and on the other side of the altar is Christ. I lay everything down on this altar. In my mind, I imagine myself kneeling before this altar, and on its table I lay all the anxiety, all the noise in my head, all the darkness I feel, all my paralyzing fear. This is my spiritual self giving up all my physical and emotional trials. As I place them on the altar, I always feel as though my burden is much lighter and my heart isn't as heavy.

The hardest part about this is the attachment with fear that abuse victims have. Fear is one of the many effects of sexual abuse. It's one of the loudest side-effects that we walk away with. It's also a wolf in sheep's clothing. Fear promotes the pretense that if we fear enough, then we'll be safe. Fear tricks us into thinking that it will be our greatest source of safety. The lie it feeds us sounds a lot like this: "If you fear everything, nothing can hurt you."

I know that you know this. It has been one of the deepest contexts of our lives. If we fear everyone, than we'll never be surprised when someone tries to hurt us. Fear feels like our superpower and also a friend. There are many times where I truly believed fear was the only thing that would watch out for me.

Throughout my life, fear has been one of the strongest muscles I've used. I would even say that at times fear was my god. Because to me, whatever consumes your mind and has the most power in your life is what you worship. What we worship with our time, thoughts, and energy is in a sense our god. And for me, fear met all those criteria. I let fear take over my thoughts, which meant that my actions were based solely on fear. I know that when I focused on my fears, I was allowing myself to sink deeper into fear's dark abyss; I wasn't letting myself experience the peace and ease that faith brings.

So to *surrender* fear feels like the equivalent of asking a warrior to go into battle without weapons. It can feel like you're giving up your best source of protection. Yet to fully receive the healing and light that are available, fear must be surrendered. As much as this idea might make you feel lost and uncertain, I promise that this is one of the most vital parts of finding the healing you're seeking.

The second principle is that of ***facing Christ***. What does that mean?

Facing Christ for me means turning my back to the fear that there are people who will hurt me and hurt those I love; instead I face only Christ. By facing Him, I allow His light to heal me, no matter what wounds I experience. I face Him and have faith that He'll always be there, always ready to heal me and to fill me with His light. This is my ultimate action of faith and my strongest weapon against fear. Since fear and faith cannot both reside within a person at the same time, I learned that I had to choose. Did I want fear or faith to rule my days?

In order to face Christ, fear had to be left behind. Facing Christ was my action step into faith. The action of facing Christ is in our mind and heart, but at times I would feel this physically. In those moments of despair and darkness, if I could imagine Christ standing there, I would face Him. I would ask Him to heal me and to take care of everything that was consuming me.

Visualizing is one of the most powerful formats I've found to help me feel as if Christ can be with me anytime and anywhere. This tool has created so much healing and peace in my life.

These two principles—surrendering fear and facing Christ—are the most important principles in the healing process. Before anything else can occur, fear must be surrendered, and faith in Christ restored.

As I walked the path of healing, there were two options. One, to believe there's no God, and that abuse is rampant simply because of the evil in this world. Or option two: to believe God not only exists but that He allows abuse to happen because of a deeper purpose that only He knows.

A life without God is something I've chosen not to live. A few years ago, when I was struggling with suicide thoughts, I decided that there was no God. I sat with that idea for a few days. Those days for me were dark and meaningless—some of the darkest and most painful days I've lived through. I then decided that this world and this life experience needed God. But mostly, *I* needed God. I desperately needed a purpose for the pain. I needed to know there was an infinite being who saw me, knew me, and had a plan for me.

From then on, I've chosen to believe in God.

That means that I would have to choose the second option. And I decided that if I was going to stay alive in a world where God doesn't stop the abuse, then I needed to learn *why* there was abuse. I was determined to understand why God would allow some of us to be abused—to see why His hand was held back and didn't protect those of us who've been through this trauma.

For many of you, I know that the trauma you went through can never be justified. There will never be anything in this world that can show you the purpose behind what you went though. I've heard many women's stories, and the pain and cruelty that runs through them can never be rectified with justice. But as you continue reading this book, as you continue in your healing process, I do believe you'll come to recognize the connection between the abuse and your greatest gifts that lie hidden within you. As you experience healing, these gifts will unfold.

I found this out for myself. As I continued to see my therapist, I began to become alive. Every week as I attended therapy, I could feel inner strength growing inside me. I began to feel the pain releasing, and as it left, a deep strength replaced it. I felt Christ's healing powers.

I find it interesting that Christ could have healed me at any time, but I first had to *choose* to be healed. And to choose to be healed means I first had to acknowledge that I was broken. Just as with a broken arm, the doctor cannot heal it unless you take the brokenness to him. Each therapy session was like a doctor's appointment with Christ. I believed He would come and help me in those sessions. I believe that He intervened when the pain was too intense for me to handle. His light was the healing salve for the wounds that seemed endless.

Soon, my paranoia went away. My anxiety decreased. Glenda taught me tools on how to lift myself out of the anxiety. So now, when anxiety struck, I had a direct path out of it. These tools, in combination with the rapid eye technology and the visualizations she walked me through, brought the beginning of change throughout my life. My children's lives were changing, and my marriage had grown stronger through my brokenness. I was beginning to see the light at the end of this tunnel.

But this was still the beginning of the path for me. There were still many principles of healing that I was to learn.

Chapter Four Journaling

What is your experience with fear?

How has fear impacted your life in the past and currently?

What would it feel like to fully surrender your fear over to Christ?

Surrender Fear, Face Christ

I want you to imagine the alter inside of your mind. I want you to then visualize taking your fear and placing it on this alter. Now, sit and journal what feelings come up for you.

_____

_____

_____

_____

_____

_____

_____

_____

_____

_____

_____

_____

_____

_____

_____

_____

_____

_____

_____

_____

Journal the emotions and thoughts that come to you around the idea of "facing Christ."

Do you believe He can heal you?
_____

Do you want to be healed?
_____

Start to write out what comes up for you with this question. For many of us, our brokenness is all that we know. Because of that, there are parts inside of us that are afraid to be healed. This is normal. Allow yourself to really be honest and truthful with this question. It will help you unlock the healing process inside of you.

_____
_____
_____
_____
_____
_____
_____
_____
_____
_____
_____
_____

The Hidden Gifts

Chapter Five
The Illusion of Protection

In the last chapter I talked a lot about fear as one of the strongest residual effects in my life from the abuse that I went through. But fear can't always be present. And when it wasn't, then its equal would be:

Control.

Control was the only way to escape the fear. Fear is exhausting, and can run your life for only periods at a time. When fear is present, our fight-or-flight mechanisms steps in. Our adrenaline picks up, and levels of stress or anxiety rise.

We can't always live in that mode. But since surrendering the fear in this moment isn't a conscious choice (as we talked about earlier), we make a subconscious choice, without ever consenting to it.

When fear steps out, something has to step in. And what decides to show up, nice and strong, is *control*.

Control is the perfect partner to fear. When control shows up, it creates the most believable illusion that you actually don't need to be afraid. It's the distorted belief that you could control all the variables in the situation and your life, and then there would be no reason to fear.

Control also clouds our vision and makes everything unclear. This is because fear is ultimately the master of control.

When control is present, there's a false comfort that fear is absent. But this is just the illusion. Control is actually the puppet to fear. Fear dictates and runs all the areas of your life that you need and want to control.

This is apparent in the life of someone who has been through any experience of sexual abuse. There's this strong belief that if we control who we're with, who our children are with, and the situations we're in, we can in fact prevent any danger or abuse from happening. This is where the control stems from. But it's like slime, dripping and oozing into all the other areas of our lives as well.

This control shows up in our marriages, our parenting, our jobs, and any other relationships we have in our life. Mostly it begins within ourselves, and that's where it is loudest.

From the moment the abuse occurred in our lives, this need to control our lives and our surroundings became a top priority. As a result, many dysfunctions begin to manifest themselves in our lives.

Many victims of abuse deal with anorexia, bulimia, self-harm, perfectionism, people pleasing, anxiety, depression, addictions, and more. These are all ways to control ourselves and our environments. These help us to cover up the pain and to feel we're no longer afraid. Instead, each one of these disfunctions are fed and pushed by the insane fear rooted deep within us.

Control is the mirage that we think will protect us.

So how do we break this illusion and let go of the fear-based control that runs each of our lives?

For me, as a survivor of sexual abuse, one of the continuing side-effects has been this inability to connect within myself and connect to others. Hugging has been one of my least favorite things to do. Keeping friendships has been very hard. And yet my deepest desire is to connect. All my heart really wants is to connect. I hate small talk, and all I desire is deep, meaningful, connected conversations with people. I want to be heard and to be loved. It's a heavy contradiction that has run my life for as long as I can remember.

Fear was the underlying theme through this contradiction. It was the background to every single day of my life. Fear and control kept me from connecting to myself and connecting to others.

There's one common piece within the need for connection and yet the reality of disconnection. That common component is pain. There's pain in the need to connect and pain in the disconnect. *Fear and control are just numbing agents to this pain.*

More so than other substances that numb, fear and control are extremely complex. They intertwine themselves into every aspect of our lives.

Pain is the reflex to fearing everything. Controlling our environment disconnects us. Fear isolates us, cornering us into a dark place that seems inescapable. And then it feels like the only way out of that dark corner is control. The need to control everything and everyone creates the illusion of safety. It makes us feel as if the fear is gone, when in reality control is just the mask that fear wears. No matter how much control you have, fear is behind it—directing or influencing every step and every move.

This pattern is one that felt impossible for me to break. It had been an impulsive, subconscious decision my whole life. How could I even imagine I could break such a strong pattern? Everywhere I turned, every relationship I had, every job, every dream—everything was laced with fear and control.

But the more I prayed and really sought the answer to this question, one word kept coming to me. And it was so simple.

Which leads us to principle number three, the principle of **connection**.

Earlier in my journey of healing, I'd seen that connection was one of the miraculous pieces to healing addictions. And here it was again. Connection was the tool that would break this pattern. Even though the fear/control muscle or reflex felt like it was made out of metal and was unbreakable, connection melted that metal.

Deep, meaningful connection to others and to oneself is powerful. It heals, it lifts pain, and it also strengthens the core emotion of love.

But how could I connect? This was the one thing I wasn't capable of doing. I'd been disconnecting my whole life, even though my main desire was to connect. I felt as if I could see the missing piece to the puzzle, but couldn't actually reach it because I was caged in. I finally knew the way out of the darkness that fear and control had made for me, but my feet were cemented to the ground. There was no movement for me.

Slowly I began to see that the more aware I was of the illusion of fear and control, the less power it had on me. I could hear when fear and control started to run my life. As soon as I could hear the fear and control, they were no longer a reflex. I had a choice in whether to let them rule my life. I envisioned my heart and saw that it was like a flower bud that had stayed closed for years. It had been waiting for the right environment and conditions to finally bloom open. I'd been hiding my heart, which in turn shut me off from connecting. As I became awake to the illusion, and could hear when fear and control were ruling me, I created a practice that I soon named "light breathing.".

Here's how it's done.

First, start by closing your eyes. Then imagine the light of Christ above your head. Take in a deep long breath, and hold in this breath for a few seconds. Then slowly let this breath out. As you slowly exhale, imagine the light of Christ flowing through you from the top of your head all the way down your body—almost like how a cup appears as it's being filled up with water, except this time it's from the top down. As His light enters your body, you'll soon be filled to the brim with light; and the light will push out all the darkness.

I use this light-breathing for more than just seeking connection. I use it for most anything I'm struggling with. But in regard to connection and letting go of fear and control, I add the visualization of light entering in and flowing through my body, so that the fear and control were pushed out. The fear and control would dissipate immediately upon contact with light. Then I would visualize the light hitting my heart and waking it up, allowing my heart to be open and available to connect. I would then ask the light to heal my heart and to help it become alive through the light of Christ, functioning as God created my heart to function—in true light, love, and deep connection.

Fear and control can make parts of us feel dead or dull. Which is why I ask for the light to make my heart become alive through the light. I ask that it be awakened to its true source of functioning, because deep meaningful connection is what we were created by God to have.

This simple exercise would push away the fear and the control and fill me with the light I was seeking. This would help me open up to connection and sink into the love that had always been waiting for me.

The more I was able to connect with myself, to God, and to my children and husband, the more I felt control slipping away. Soon I could feel that I was able to make decisions from a place of love and confidence instead of fear.

It was uncomfortable at first, since fear had been such a necessary companion for me. But eventually I was able to wipe my lenses through which I'd always viewed life. Things became more clear. The life that had once been tainted with the color and flavor of fear and control was now marked in love.

If I start to disconnect from my loved ones, the old patterns of fear and control show up again, every single time. So this is a lifelong practice for me. I have to keep myself awake and present to continue to choose connection over disconnection. To choose to trust in God instead of worshiping at the altar of fear and control.

Chapter Five Journaling

How does control affect your life? What areas of your life do you find the need for control?

The Illusion of Protection

Do you find it hard to deeply connect to those you love?

_____

What scares you about being connected to others?

The Illusion of Protection

What inspires you about being connected?

Practice doing the "Light Breathing" and then journal your experience.

The Illusion of Protection

Chapter Six
Run. Stuff. Numb it.

Running. Stuffing pain. Numbing.

Do any of these sound familiar?

Most likely they do. Because this is the pattern for victims of abuse.

We run. We run from pain or discomfort at the slightest prick.

Do you ever wonder why you want to quit life so often? Or why the conversation of divorce floods your mind when in reality you have a decent marriage?

Jobs. How many have you had? How often do you run from them at the first sight of discomfort or confrontation?

Confrontation. That word alone has sent stress and anxiety straight through to my brain on numerous occasions. I've run from it in every situation possible.

I once bought a luxurious and expensive couch. It took three months for them to make and deliver it. My family sat in lawn chairs in our living room for three months until this beautiful new couch arrived. The day finally came, and the couch was delivered. I was beyond excited—until I realized they'd made the couch in the wrong material. And not only was it wrong, it was the one material I'd said I did *not* want for the couch.

We'd saved our money for a long time before we were able to buy this couch. Then we'd waited patiently for three months to finally put it into our home. When it came to us in the wrong fabric, I had every right to call and complain.

If you feel the way I've felt about confrontation, you know how my couch story ends.

I never opened my mouth. I didn't call them. Actually, I think I told them how happy I was with the couch. To avoid looking bad and picky, I lied. I lied to run away from any form of confrontation.

This is just one story out of millions in my life. I've avoided or run away from anything that might cause pain or discomfort.

If a relationship or friendship hit a level of pain I didn't want to deal with, I cut that friendship off faster than scissors cutting string.

That friend, that relationship, was gone to me. I would rather have been alone than deal with the pain or problem that was showing up in the relationship.

How I've managed to stay married for fifteen years is truly a miracle. It's the only relationship I've been able to keep alive for that long.

Pain has always equaled *I run*.

We run from it. And—we stuff it.

Stuffing pain deep down. I'm sure you know what I mean. Because if we didn't do this, as survivors of sexual abuse, we would die every day from the pain we haven't dealt with.

Stuffing the pain has proven to be a God-sent blessing. It makes life more bearable and also more livable.

At the same time, stuffing the pain is a two-edged sword.

Because it means that all that stuffed-down pain will one day fly out.

Imagine the closet you've seen in the movies (or in your home) that's stuffed and filled to the top with storage and crap. When someone opens the door to that closet, all the junk spills out. Without the door there holding it in, it can't be contained anymore.

The Hidden Gifts

The crap is coming out. It's inevitable, no matter how hard anyone tries to stop it.

If we don't clean out the crap in our closet, then we also don't have a choice on when the crap spills out.

How many times have you been in a situation that was hard but not really *that* hard—maybe a little disagreement with your loved one or spouse, maybe someone using a certain tone or saying something hurtful—and instead of being just a little angry or hurt, the door to the closet got opened, and all your hidden pain unleashed.

Instead of your pain being at a level three or four, which is what you'd expect from an incident that small, you've hit twenty on a one-to-ten scale.

Can you see how this has been your experience?

What's so brutal about it is that we don't even know how the door to our pain closet got opened. We start to believe that certain relationships or situations must be toxic and bad because of the level of pain we feel. Which is why most of us run from relationships and friendships. We run from what feels bad and painful. When the insane reality is that the source of our pain is actually *inside* us. It's within the vault of pain we carry around wherever we go. In essence we're running from pain that we think is being caused outside ourselves, yet is actually within us. We end up running in circles like the dog chasing his tail. Always moving, always running, never getting anywhere.

There's a good chance that some of your relationships and friendships may seem toxic. But if your closet and vault of pain were cleaned up, you would be able to be present in the moment and to see the relationship more clearly.

Cleaning out the pain closet is one of the hardest things you'll ever do, and also the most beneficial.

When we aren't running or stuffing we numb it.

We've all been to the dentist and had a shot of Lidocaine to numb our mouth. We're all familiar with this feeling. Most of us probably hate this feeling.

I hate how the numbing makes it impossible to fully function in that area of my mouth. When I get my mouth numbed, I can't eat, I can't smile, and I can't even talk well.

The Lidocaine protected me from the pain of the dental work, but for the next four hours it prevented my mouth from functioning in the way it was made to function.

In the case of the dental work, I'm grateful for the numbing. It's a benefit.

Actually in the case of the pain from sexual abuse, I'm also grateful for numbing agents. There were times in my life where I wasn't able to handle or deal with the pain I felt. I turned primarily to sugar and caffeine as my numbing agents. Being over-busy and highly distracted have always helped to numb me as well, and I have a great amount of gratitude for the help they've given me through the years when I wasn't capable of dealing with my pain. As with all things, I believe they serve a purpose in our lives.

Numbing agents can be helpful in our darkest of times. But when you find yourself using narcotics and alcohol for their numbing effect, you've now added a new backpack of problems onto your life. I do believe we must all numb out at times. But turning to drugs or alcohol will not only numb you but also steal you away from the healing path you're gifted to walk on. They prevent you from moving forward. They keep you stuck in addictions that hijack your agency and your ability to make choices. Action is hard to take when under the influence of these numbing agents. Which is why I believe they prevent you from moving forward on the path of healing and uncovering your gifts.

The downside to numbing our pain is that we can't fully function. Just as with the Lidocaine, we won't function how were created to function.

Our feelings of joy and happiness will be numbed just as much as our feelings of pain and suffering. By numbing the pain, we shut off the joy that's available for us to feel.

Also, if we let the pain get strong enough instead of numbing it, we'll eventually seek out the help we need. It took me two months of hell and pain to finally seek help from a therapist. Money, time, nothing mattered anymore; nothing stood in my way to receiving help. I was going to find help to relieve the pain and insanity that was ruling my life.

This is the benefit of allowing ourselves to feel the pain.

If you broke your leg but were still able to walk without pain, you might not seek out help to have your leg healed. But since you can't walk on a broken leg, and even the best painkillers can't take away that kind of physical pain, you'll find a hospital and a doctor who can help fix the fracture.

Same principle here with the pain of abuse.

Sometimes we don't have the tools, support, or emotional stability to deal with our pain. And that's when we use our reactionary tools of running, stuffing, and numbing.

When you're ready, or even when you're not, the right time will come to heal.

I didn't think I was going to finally address my abuse pain; I thought I'd already addressed it! Until one day it hit me hard, and I fell flat on my face.

Other women I've talked to woke up one day, and the memories of their abuse came flooding back. There was no longer any turning away from it.

No matter how or when it's time for you to deal with this closet of pain, it will show up, and it *will* happen.

And you'll get the opportunity to stop running, stop stuffing, and stop numbing.

When you do, hell will break loose, and your healing will come.

Which leads me to a fourth principle: **be awake, and be willing**.

The more you choose to be awake to all that I've addressed so far, the more you'll be able to heal and receive the gifts waiting for you as you walk the path of healing. If you can be willing and open to healing, the process will rush over you like water. There'll be moments of intensity. There'll be roads that are unknown and dark. But when you're willing, the light will come, and the healing can take place.

Chapter Six Journaling

How do you run? What are some ways that you run from the pain? If you run away from relationships, what are the triggers that make you run?

_____

_____

_____

_____

_____

_____

_____

_____

_____

_____

_____

_____

_____

_____

_____

_____

_____

_____

_____

_____

_____

_____

_____

_____

The Hidden Gifts

Start to look in your life and see how you "stuff" your pain. Do you deal with confrontations, or do you stuff them instead to avoid dealing with the problem?

Journal around incidents where you avoid confrontations and upsets.

How do you numb your pain? Start to watch in your life for when pain hits. When the pain shows up, what do you turn to?

Or, for a backwards effect, when you start to turn to an addiction, look and see what triggered you to use that numbing agent.

The Hidden Gifts

When we numb our pain, we also numb our joy and happiness. How does that make you feel when you realize that it is the numbing that also steals your joy?

Chapter Seven
Protecting the Monster

Almost all the survivors I've talked with have one trait in common. It's the piece that holds the most pain, and that also keeps the vile monster of sexual abuse alive.

It's the insane need to protect our abusers, or protect those we love.

If this didn't exist, then every sexual abuse case would be shared, every abuser reported. This is the source of the problem of why millions of abusers go unnoticed. Someone feels the need or the fear to protect them.

How else can you explain the wife who doesn't report that her husband has been abusing their children?

Why else would a five-year-old not tell her mom about the babysitter molesting her?

You could ask this question for every abuse story you hear. *Why* did this incident go untold? *Why* did it get hidden and brushed under the rug?

It's the incessant need to protect the abuser or to protect those connected to the victim who might be hurt by this information. This is what causes so much pain and so many repeat abuses.

The hiding causes the deep pain. There's a fear that the abuser will be in trouble with the law. Or even the fear that no one will believe you when you tell about the abuse. As I've spoken with many women about their stories, I've heard many say how their abusers threatened to hurt their family if they ever told. This is extremely and heartbreakingly common. It creates a deep fear and a need to protect the secret of the abuse. Abusers know that what they're doing is wrong, and they'll do anything to not be found out.

There's so much need for the victim to protect the monster of abuse.

I know that this is why I didn't tell my parents about my abuse for so long. I was afraid to tell on my babysitter. I was afraid of what might happen to her or to me if I did.

Would I get into trouble? Would she get into trouble? As a five-year-old, I was uncertain as to who was responsible for this behavior going on.

This thread of protecting the abuser and the abuse weaves its way through many instances.

One woman told me her story of being a young girl when she was abused. Her mother had to send her to a babysitter's house regularly because of serious health problems her father was having. It was at the babysitter's house that she was abused. She told me she would make sure her little sisters were outside so they wouldn't get abused. She decided at that young age to suffer the abuse in order to protect her siblings. She said that even to this day she would never tell anyone about the abuse she received because it would hurt her mother.

This is who we are as victims and survivors of abuse.

I believe we all were born with a strong desire to help others. And when the abuse occurred, that trait inside us got amped up but also tainted.

We feel this unhinged need to help and protect others—our abuser, as well as others we love and don't want to get hurt.

While still young, we decide that we'll take the abuse to protect someone else. Many of us have felt this strongly—this innate sense that we're strong enough to take on the abuse and all its dark effects. Because of the fear of others' reactions, we would never want anyone to know what we've been through. We don't want their pity or their sympathy. There's a fear that others will see us differently if they knew what we'd been exposed to. So we stuff all this inside us and live behind a facade of strength, a pretense that we ourselves believe in.

The idea of protecting the monster of abuse became very personal for me when I found out that my abuser's father was in jail for child molestation. In that moment, my perspective shifted. I gained a higher view of life. I was able to see beyond the trees that had always been in my way. I realized that my abuser was most likely abused by her own father.

A powerful wave of clarity rushed over me.

And then, deep empathy filled me. Empathy for her. How horrible it must've been for her to be abused by her father. My heart ached for her.

As I've been vocal about my platform of sexual abuse advocacy, I've felt like I was "coming out of the closet" to the world. My darkest secret was now being aired for anyone and everyone to know. This brought a few circumstances that were pretty uncomfortable for me. I was with one person who had known me as a child and lived in my neighborhood, and who knew my abuser as well as others who had babysat me. You can agree with me that knowing my abuser's identity was none of this person's business—but agree also that it didn't really matter if they knew. Yet this fear engulfed me. I couldn't let out my abuser's name.

How was it that thirty years later, I still felt this heavy pull to protect my abuser?

"*No one* can know!" This is the sentence that kept running through my mind, over and over. Anxiety seized my chest, and I found it hard to breathe.

And then I saw it. I saw this crazy madness.

I was feeling the need to protect the secret—the monster of abuse.

We protect our abusers. And it's because of this that abuse continues. It continues through many people. And it runs like a dark muddy river that goes underground. No light, no truth, no speaking of it.

As it continues to be hidden, protected, and ignored, it will seep through generation upon generation, down the family line. It's an emotional baggage that gets passed along, time and time again. The secrets hold power, and fear grips the victims.

So how do we heal this?

This leads us to principle number five: **we must speak our truth**.

I don't care if your abuse happened fifty years ago or this past year, you must speak it out. Acknowledge that it actually happened to you.

Speak it out for the sweet little child who still lives somewhere deep in your subconscious, waiting to be validated. This version of you who has been shamed, ignored, and stuffed down for as long as you can remember. Acknowledge this part of you, and what that part of you went through. See the pain, name the pain, and hear the pain.

Speak your truth to someone who will hear you.

This most likely will mean you need to spend the money and take the time to see a therapist, if only so that you can be heard by someone who will hear and believe you. Because *you are worth it*.

Spend the money. Take the time. Validate what has happened to you.

And then we must speak out. We must teach our children so they'll never be shamed and never in trouble.

Over and over, we're to let our children know we're here to protect them. Teaching them that they're not alone in this life. Assuring them that they don't need to bear full responsibility for keeping themselves safe.

Promising that we'll always do the best we can to watch over them and protect them.

Then telling them that we can't always protect them, even if we try every second of the day. We must teach them that these things called abuse are not okay—but if it happens to them, they'll never be shamed. They'll always be loved.

I want you now to do something for the part inside you that took the abuse. Imagine someone standing before you—and that person is *you* at whatever age you were abused.

You tell this person all these things: affirm that she (or he) is not in trouble; reassure her that she's loved; and most of all, state the truth that the abuse wasn't her fault.

Tell her how sad you are that she wasn't protected. Let her know that from now on she *will* be protected.

Speak to her in a way that you'd wished someone had talked to you back when your abuse had occured. Imagine that piece of you, and just hug that version of you in your mind.

This is where we can begin. Healing our inner self. Beginning with our own pain, our own darkness.

The idea of trying to stop abuse is like wishing the sun would be purple. Sexual abuse has always been here, and as the world continues to be plagued with pornography and filth, it will only become worse. Unless we raise our voices and blast the world with our truth.

We must teach. We must share. We must lift our voice so that our words may guide and help other survivors. Our sharing is a gift to all who are currently drowning in the dark. As we unite, light will grow. And as a small light bulb can light even the darkest of rooms, so can even our small lights set this world on fire.

Chapter Seven Journaling

How have you hidden the monster of abuse? What are your fears around others finding out that you were abused?

I want you to write down what you said to that part inside of you – the part that went through the abuse.

Let yourself say all of the things you wish that someone had said to you. Allow yourself to feel these words rush over you and begin to heal your heart, validating who you are and what you went through.

Protecting the Monster

Chapter Eight
Ask and Receive

If you're still angry at God for not protecting you or those you love, know that I hear you. I believe that acknowledging this anger is a crucial part in the healing process. It's important for you to not make yourself wrong for this. Allow yourself the space to be angry at God.

For many of us who are raised in a religious settings, the idea of being angry at God is a shameful one. Most likely if you were to voice those feelings, you would be condemned and labeled as wrong. There's so much fear in our anger toward God.

But holding in those feelings will only push Him farther away. Allowing yourself the space to acknowledge the anger and hatred you have toward Him will break down the walls you've put up. These walls are keeping Him at a far distance from you.

The painful stories I've heard from women and their abuse trauma always brings up anger for me. I still don't have a complete understanding of why God has allowed such horrific things to occur to such innocent children. I go through waves of hatred and love with God. It's a wave that rushes in and out depending on where I am at that time.

But there's an underlying love, a holy and sacred love that I hold for God. And giving myself the space to hate Him at times also gives me more access to Him, because I choose not to keep the wall up anymore. When we're dishonest with ourselves, we hold God at arm's length. We're the ones who keep Him distant. We hold the power to allow Him in or to push Him away.

God is always there. He's waiting for us to finally unlock the doors and take down the walls so that we may fully receive all that He has for us.

Christ has made this promise: "Ask, and it shall be given you; seek, and ye shall find; knock, and it shall be opened unto you: for every one that asketh receiveth; and he that seeketh findeth; and to him that knocketh it shall be opened" (Matthew 7:7-8).

I encourage you to talk to God. Even if that means yelling at Him. But don't shut Him out. He's the leader of light for your path. He's the only one who can truly show you how to heal. It's in His words and His guidance that you'll find the key to peace and your own rebirth.

You may believe that God doesn't speak to you. You may think that I must be special or different because of what I've experienced. But I'll tell you that I'm no different from you, except that I've always believed God speaks to us. I believe He will speak to anyone and guide anyone, if they'll open their mind and ears to hear Him.

You don't need to be holy or righteous to hear His words. You need no title or calling to allow yourself to hear God. *You* are enough. The battered, broken mess that you are is *enough*.

When Christ came to this earth, He didn't sit with the church leaders. He didn't sit with the holy and righteous people. Instead He came and sat with the sinners. He was there to save those who needed to be saved. Christ came to heal those who were willing to be saved.

Principle number six is this: ***be open and willing to hear God.***

Willing is a crucial word here. I've always thought I had to be perfect to be loved or to be healed. This was one of the traits I took on from my abuse. I like to call it the perfectionism defect. I had this false sense of reality where I thought I had to be perfect to be cleansed from the abuse that had occurred to me. I also believed I had to be perfect to ever be loved again. Especially by God and Christ.

But this couldn't be more false. It isn't that we need to be more perfect, but that we need to be more willing. More willing to open up our wounds and let them be the mess and pain that they are. Willing to look at where we're broken, and to sit within the brokenness. And then most of all, the ultimate surrender of being willing to let God and Christ into our hearts, and allowing them to really love us, even if we may feel damaged and broken.

Christ is the salve to our wounds. He is our healing agent. He is our hope and our light.

At times in my life I've felt that the pain had hit a level I couldn't bear any longer. And not just on the day when I'd decided not to live. Many times over throughout my life, I've felt high levels of emotional pain. When that pain got too high, and too hard to hold, I've found that if I sought out Christ through prayer, the pain would subside. It would dissipate, like mist rising to the sky. I could feel it leave me; warmth would pour over me and fill me instead. This is how I know that Christ is the healing agent: I've felt His healing power many times in my life.

I know it may feel scary to pray and ask Christ to heal this pain you're currently in. I understand the doubts and fears you may have. I can feel the insecurity around your ability to receive. But I promise that if you have belief and hope, you'll begin to receive from God, and you'll be able to experience this relief and guidance I'm speaking of.

Chapter Eight Journaling

Are you angry with God? Have you ever let yourself feel this anger before? Do you feel that He abandoned you by not protecting you from the abuse? Do you believe that He loves you? Begin here by just simply writing. Start writing everything that comes from asking yourself these questions. Let it flow, and don't make yourself wrong for how you feel.

The Hidden Gifts

Ask and Receive

Do you believe that God speaks to us on this earth?

_____

_____

_____

_____

_____

_____

Do you believe that He can speak to you?

_____

_____

_____

_____

_____

_____

_____

_____

_____

_____

_____

_____

What experiences have you had with hearing God? Take a minute to look back and see if and when God has spoken to you.

Ask and Receive

Are you open and willing to hear God?

_____

_____

_____

Have you ever felt your pain be taken away when asking through prayer? If so, write that experience down. If not, do you have a desire for this to happen?

_____

_____

_____

_____

_____

_____

_____

_____

_____

_____

_____

_____

_____

_____

_____

_____

_____

_____

_____

_____

_____

_____

_____

_____

_____

Are you willing to ask for that to happen?

_____

_____

_____

_____

I want you to write out WHAT life would be like for you IF you were led by God daily.

How would that feel for you?

Ask and Receive

The best way to start hearing God is to wake up to the inspiration we receive. To do that, begin writing down ANY form of inspiration you receive throughout the day (even if it's as small as a feeling to turn off the stove when you feel inspiration to do so). Write here any form of inspiration you receive this week.

The Hidden Gifts

_____

_____

_____

_____

_____

_____

_____

_____

_____

_____

_____

_____

_____

_____

_____

_____

_____

_____

_____

_____

By doing this practice, you tune into the spiritual guidance you are already receiving. This then allows you to receive more spiritual guidance daily.

Chapter Nine
Your Greatest Weapon

The next two principles offer important help in the process of receiving from God. These two principles are simply: **believe** and **hope**.

Believing is where our intention and our strength come from. Belief is one of the most powerful tools we could ever access. It's the source of our willpower when we're learning a skill or pushing ourselves to be greater. Belief is the glue that holds us together when we're climbing. The belief that there'll be a top to the mountain, and that the climb was worth it. The same principle applies here with God. If we truly believe that He will hear and give to us, that belief will call it forward.

You must also have hope that there's a God. You must cling to the hope that all your pain can and will bring forth goodness and healing, and that there's more to this world than the darkness you've experienced.

If you were going into battle, you would want the best weapons possible, weapons that would give you the most protection and be the strongest against your opponents.

The battle we march into every day as survivors looks very different from those taking place on a battlefield. Our battles are wars and contentions within our own minds.

Most of those battles are drenched in hopelessness and unbelief. Which is why the principle of hope is our greatest weapon as we deal with the emotional war raging inside us.

Hopelessness is equivalent to being stranded in a lifeboat in the middle of the ocean—without a destination. There's no plan on how to find land. Instead, you're stuck in this sea of water.

How long can you last? How long will it be before you die in the middle of this ocean? There's no reason to hurriedly paddle because you have no idea where you're going, or if paddling fast is even worth it. This is hopelessness.

But if you had hope that land wasn't far away, you would find yourself driven to find it. Hope for the land that's waiting for you will pull you onward through the waves and through the heat of a scorching sun. Hope will give you the endurance to push through hunger and exhaustion. Hope will do all this because the destination you're seeking is a magnet for you. It pulls you to paddle harder, to move forward faster. Hope brings you to your destination. There's hope that you'll survive, that you'll arrive on land once again.

As victims and survivors of abuse, hope has been tainted, warped, and most times lost. Hope for a life without pain might seem like a mirage that can never be real. The hope that you can heal and find joy might seem unattainable.

But if hope is our greatest weapon, how do you get that hope? How do you plant the seeds of hope within yourself? When all seems lost and unsure, how do you even find those seeds? How could you even imagine that land could show up after being stuck so long on that lifeboat?

How is it even possible to hope that one day you might be on the other side of this pain?

The answer to this *how* is *yes*. There is no how; it's just *yes*. Yes to finding the destination that lies within your mind. Yes to hope. Yes to hope that you can live without the darkness and despair in your life. Yes to hope that you'll no longer suffer nights filled with loneliness, pain, and disconnection.

Once you're a yes for hope, seeds of hope will be planted within your mind. These seeds will grow into deeply rooted trees. Yes, you'll be like a tree planted firmly, with roots that go down deep into fertile soil. So when the winds of pain and uncertainty come, they'll be only for your good, strengthening your roots and giving you the space to grow taller and flourish.

Let the wind and the storms be the elements that foster your growth instead of breaking you.

You see, darkness tricks us into thinking it has won. Depression, anxiety, fear, sadness, loneliness, suicidal thoughts, trauma, grief—all these dark clouds looming over our heads will trick us into thinking we've lost. That we've lost our belief in who we are and what we're supposed to do. The heaviness of these experiences taint our vision and suck out our hope. The more you lose hope, the louder these feelings become. The louder they get, the more we believe they've won, that we're too weak to fight against them. Despair and resignation can begin to fill us.

Yet if we stand back a bit, and see this only for the trick that it is, we regain the power of agency in our world. The light within us that's suffocated can inhale deeply again. And hope will return. As hope returns, the noise of these overwhelming feelings will subside into the background, and eventually be silenced altogether.

Hope is our weapon against this lie. It's the piece that opens our eyes, awakens our hearts, and ultimately *saves our lives*. For some of us, that's literal; for others it's only a metaphor. A metaphor that this hope will save them from a life of despair and loneliness. But hope will allow you to live the life where you're awake. Awake to the joy, awake to the love, awake to yourself.

Hope saved my life that February afternoon. Hope continues to save my life. Each time the suicidal thoughts get loud, if I can ask God for hope, hope saves me. That tiny glimmer of light has kept me walking when everything inside me wanted to stay in the dark. It's the belief that things aren't always as they seem. The belief that pain and breakdown are always a precursor to growth and breakthroughs.

If you can access the power of hope, you'll begin to share hope. Light is then shared, and light is in return received.

All of this by being a *yes*.

A yes doesn't need a reason or proof. A yes is a yes.

Be a yes, and be open to hope. Pray to God that He'll bless you with hope.

This is where I began. During those times of pain and darkness, I asked God to bless me with hope. I asked Him to send down hope to wake up my true self. As I did, I found myself being open to hope. I was a yes. And when I decided to be a yes, it was if I chose to turn on a faucet. I opened my heart and my mind and allowed God to pour His hope down on me, washing away the fear and the darkness. When that happened, it was as if someone had changed the prescription on my glasses. Life appeared differently to me.

Hope shifts the way you view life.

James R. Sherman writes: "You can't go back and make a new start, but you can start right now and make a brand new ending."

This is what hope does. It allows you to let go of the past, and to hope and create a better future. You get to change the ending of your story. No one has their story concrete and finite. Yet this is how most of us live life. We believe our life must end in a certain way, a set way, because of the abuse we went through.

Hope changes our ending. We have the opportunity to seek out and create a new ending. Or even better, a new beginning to the life we're currently living.

Hope is the secret weapon that's often misjudged and forgotten.

If you want to change your life, if you want to escape the darkness and pain that now consumes your life, seek out hope. Focus your energy on building anew, and on creating the life you want to live.

Allow the hope to direct you toward that land. Cling to the hope, and soon it will begin to show up as belief. And when you believe, your actions will bring forth new results and new feelings.

Confidence and peace will replace the worry and fear. Darkness cannot exist within the presence of light. Therefore, the more hope and belief you can have, the more light you'll experience. As darkness slips away, the light becomes stronger.

What if we could view our abuse differently? What if we could view that experience through a sharper lens, one that allows us to see the whole instead of the fragment?

Abraham Lincoln said, "We can complain that rose bushes have thorns, or rejoice because thorn bushes have roses."

Could life really be altered just by how we view it? Could the hope for something better or brighter actually pull us from our moments of hell?

Miracles begin with a simple yes to hope.

The more you seek it, the more it will show up. And soon enough, belief will follow, strengthening your roots and spreading your branches.

Little by little.

Hold onto your hope. And let that hope sprout into a faith that will carry you forward.

That faith will grow, and you'll be able to see, little by little, the fruits of your faith. God will speak to you. He will guide you. You'll begin to feel His grace flow around your and your life.

Chapter Nine Journaling

Begin by writing out your hopelessness. Clean it all out. Write out all the areas of your life where you feel hopeless and lost.

Your Greatest Weapon

Now start writing what you hope for in this life. Allow yourself to really dive in and dream. What is your greatest hope and desire?

_____

_____

_____

_____

_____

_____

_____

_____

_____

_____

_____

_____

_____

_____

_____

_____

_____

_____

_____

_____

The Hidden Gifts

Now ask yourself if you believe this can happen?

The Hidden Gifts

Start creating how life would look life for you if you were armed with the weapons of hope and belief. What would your everyday look like? What does your future look like?

_____
_____
_____
_____
_____
_____
_____
_____
_____
_____
_____
_____
_____
_____
_____
_____
_____
_____
_____
_____
_____

Your Greatest Weapon

What does it feel like to say, "I am a YES to hope!"

_____
_____
_____
_____
_____
_____
_____
_____
_____
_____
_____
_____
_____
_____

I want you to grab a separate piece of paper and write these words in BOLD letters:

I AM A YES FOR HOPE!!

Now, tape this paper up somewhere in your home where you will see it often. You might want to make a few of them. The purpose for this exercise is so that you can see these words and say them over and over in your mind. This will help you create the space for hope to grow, daily!

Write out a new ending for your life, one that isn't dictated by the abuse you went through. Create a new ending to live into; one that is created from the place of HOPE.

_____

_____

_____

_____

_____

_____

_____

_____

_____

_____

_____

_____

_____

_____

_____

_____

_____

_____

_____

_____

_____

_____

The Hidden Gifts

Chapter Ten
How Abuse Looks Every Day

Each of us has our own story.

Every one reading this book has their own detailed story of abuse.

Your story may have been with you for most of your life. Or you were granted the gift of forgetting, and then one day, those memories came flooding back.

Whether you've remembered it your whole life, or the memories have recently surfaced, the effects of the abuse has permeated every decision and every relationship in your life.

The more I share and write about the effects of abuse, the more women reach out to me. As they would talk to me about their experiences with abuse, they would tell me the same thing: "When I read your words, Keira, I feel like I'm reading my own words."

This has confirmed what I've felt all along: that we're all so much alike. The pain I've felt from my abuse experience is the same as your pain from your own personal abuse. The fear, the terror, the panic, the schizophrenia—all the same. So how is it that we've all felt so alone?

Being alone is the biggest tragedy in all this.

Because sexual abuse is hidden, and shoved down into the dark, this is how each victim feels.

We feel hidden. There's a feeling of being forgotten, unseen, and not validated.

The grief that comes from feeling unheard and having a lack of support is immeasurable. The truth is, those who love us and take care of us don't know how to hear us or support us.

If they'd been through abuse themselves, more than likely your own abuse just triggered all their pain. The despair they feel because abuse occurred for you will cloud their vision. They won't be able to see you. All they'll be able to see is their own pain, their own fears becoming true. They'll be overtaken by the guilt of having failed to protect you.

As they deal with their own strangling hell, you'll be left there. *Alone*. Wondering why you aren't being taken care of. You'll sit there in your own battered emotions and begin to realize that you must be the one to take care of yourself. This is the beginning of your journey of feeling alone. From that moment, you'll learn the survival techniques for being alone.

Or there's the case in which the loved one you're speaking to about your abuse will have zero context on how to help you. If they don't seek out help from a professional, they'll try to help you from the context of their own life—which will be something along the lines of blaming you, shaming you, and making you wrong.

Sometimes it will be that you're just not believed. They don't want to imagine that you actually had to go through that abuse. Or since most predators are family members or close friends, they won't be able to believe the story. It's a heartbreaking reality to think that someone you love is a sexual predator. There's nothing more life-altering or ground-shaking than to find out that the abuser is someone they've loved and trusted.

Trust. This is the word that doesn't live in our worlds or in the world of abuse.

When we're young, we easily learn to trust. We must. We have to trust that our parents will feed us, protect us, and guide us in this world we're so new to. We don't even have an idea of the cruelty and evil in this world. We know only the things that we grow up with.

I would hope that many of you readers grew up in a fairly functional family, and were abused outside of that family unit. But I know too well to assume such a thing. I'm aware that many of you were born into the hell of abuse. I know that there are far too many who experience the debilitating affect of incestual sexual abuse. That's truly a hell you cannot escape. And for you, my heart breaks. I pray that all the healing powers of heaven will pour over you as you walk your healing path.

Whatever your experience was growing up, you naturally trusted those who raised you. You were taught to trust family members and friends. I'm sure you were taught and trained when to run from strangers or stay away from people you don't know. But most of us aren't taught to listen to our gut. Not many children are taught to stay away from people who make them feel bad, whether it be their grandpa, uncle, dad, sister, or another family member. Instead, we're pushed to love them. We're taught to ignore that feeling of warning in our guts and continue to be with them and spend time with them. This practice is one that makes us deny our divine gift of discernment. The more we ignore it and deny the power it has for us, the more we live off-center. Our choices and the people in our life stop being chosen by our discernment. Which creates a life of havoc within our souls.

As children, our hearts and minds are open. We believe. We trust. We have faith and hope. This is why Christ tells us in the Scriptures to become as a little child. We're pure when we're children.

So when abuse occurs for us, we begin to question our ability to trust. We start to make ourselves wrong for trusting the abuser. Or we stop trusting those who were supposed to protect us. We don't trust their judgment or their ability to raise us.

This is why many victims of abuse are so independent. At a young age, they choose to become their own protector. No longer trusting the adults in their lives to keep them safe, they decide to be their own guardian.

And now—ten, twenty, thirty years later—you can sit back and see the effects of this rippling through each part of your life. This is why you can't trust even those you love most. This is why you're so independent, never letting anyone carry your load or burden. These moments in your past dictate each and every part of your current life. *Trust* is a word that's not in your vocabulary. You tell yourself that it's dangerously naive to trust. No one is your protector or your guardian.

How does this affect your life? Were you eventually able to get married? How did that marriage work? Did you push away your spouse at the slightest feeling of distrust? Were there walls you refused to let your spouse through? Did you end up divorced—perhaps because your trust in your spouse was violated, or maybe because you never let your spouse in?

How is your relationship with your kids? Do you fear connecting to them? Or maybe you want so badly to connect, but you keep hitting a wall of disconnect. Then the plague of loneliness continues to fall upon your life and your family. The effects of loneliness and disconnect tear away the light and the life within you and those around you.

Disconnect is the theme of life for most sexual abuse victims. I personally believe it's because we learned to disconnect in order to survive the abuse. By disconnecting to the abuser and the abuse, we were able to live. So it became a part of us. *Disconnect = living*.

Interestingly, in my life I've seen this play out in two ways. The first is that I can connect very easily with people. It's one of my natural gifts. If you meet me, you most likely will feel a connection with me. On the flip side, if you're close to me in my life, then there's a disconnect that happens. Although I connect easily to those who come into my life for a brief time, it has been the hardest thing to become deeply connected to those I love most.

I've seen the exhausting effects this has had in my marriage and in my children's lives. They've all struggled because I was unable to connect. I remember really trying hard to sit and connect with my children and being unable to. I would end up getting up and doing mindless chores like laundry.

In my marriage, I never let my husband do anything for me. My deep need to be independent and to protect myself left a gaping hole in our relationship.

As I was thrown into my healing path, I began to see the beautiful results of connection.

I saw how connecting was and continues to be the most vital and important principle in my life.

First, as I became broken and needed my husband to carry me, I was finally able to connect with him. Fifteen years of marriage, and it took my breaking to allow him in past my walls of independence and my protective shell. Our emotional and spiritual connection became my greatest source of joy. And it has continued to grow and strengthen since that space of brokenness.

One of the greatest blessings and joys from the healing I've been able to experience has been the connection developing with my kids. For the first time in their lives, they've been able to connect with me, their mother! And as I've been available to connect, to hear and to love them, they've flourished. Misguided behaviors they had for years started to dissipate. We began to feel as if miracles were being poured out onto our family.

You may not have the motivation to start looking into your pain and allowing yourself to heal. But your children and their happiness will be directly affected.

I know this won't be an easy path for you. I know there are many obstacles in your way.

I also know the absolute miracles that will shower upon those you love, as well as in your own life, when you take the leap forward and find help with your healing.

Chapter Ten Journaling

What was your experience when you told the first person about your abuse? How did they react? Most importantly, what were the feelings you had when they reacted?

_____

_____

_____

_____

_____

_____

_____

_____

_____

_____

_____

_____

_____

_____

_____

_____

_____

_____

_____

_____

How Abuse Looks Every Day

Now look at THOSE feelings. Can you see how those feelings have been the underlying crust to most of your life? Write about how and where those feelings occur for you currently in your life.

_____
_____
_____
_____
_____
_____
_____
_____
_____
_____
_____
_____
_____
_____
_____
_____
_____
_____
_____
_____

The Hidden Gifts

Have you felt your "divine gift of discernment?" If you have, do you listen to it? What happens when you listen to it, and when you don't listen to it?

What have you experienced with trust? Do you trust easily? Is it very hard for you to trust?

What are your relationships with loved ones like? Do you allow yourself to trust them? Do you allow them in emotionally?

Let's now address the concept of ***Disconnect***. Can you look back in your life and see if you started to disconnect after your abuse? Did you start to pull away from those you loved?

_____
_____
_____
_____
_____
_____
_____
_____
_____
_____
_____
_____
_____
_____
_____
_____
_____
_____
_____
_____

Did the disconnect occur for you when you first told someone about the abuse you had gone through? This experience of sharing about your abuse to someone else can be where most of the trauma occurs. There is a good possibility that this was the moment when you first began to disconnect. Write about how that experience was for you.

Can you feel how disconnect has been a way for you to not feel the shame and guilt that comes from the abuse? The disconnect has been a vital way to live life without the heaviness of shame.

The Hidden Gifts

I want you to really be honest with yourself and write how disconnect shows up in your life. Where does it play a role in your marriage, romantic relationships, parenting, friends, work, etc.? Do you find that it shows up everywhere?

How Abuse Looks Every Day

Can you also see how disconnect has kept you from the love and joy you have always wanted?

_____

_____

_____

_____

_____

_____

_____

_____

_____

_____

_____

_____

_____

_____

_____

_____

_____

_____

_____

_____

Loneliness. This is the direct result of disconnection. This is what we get instead of the love an joy the connection brings. So, let's look at how loneliness affects our lives.

When do you feel lonely? How does loneliness feel in your mind and body? What do you do when you feel that loneliness come upon you? How do you deal with the loneliness? Start to listen to your thoughts when loneliness occurs.

The Hidden Gifts

When do you feel connected? When do you let yourself feel love and give love? What does that experience feel like for you?

_____

_____

_____

_____

_____

_____

_____

_____

_____

_____

_____

_____

_____

_____

_____

_____

_____

_____

_____

_____

The Hidden Gifts

How Abuse Looks Every Day

I want you to now create how each area of your life would look and feel *if* you were *connected*.

_____
_____
_____
_____
_____
_____
_____
_____
_____
_____
_____
_____
_____
_____
_____
_____
_____
_____
_____
_____

The Hidden Gifts

Chapter Eleven
Are There Really Hidden Gifts Inside This Hell?

Yes.

There really are hidden gifts inside this crap. But they're not easy to see, which is why I say they're hidden. If they were just out in the open ready to be seen and accessed, they wouldn't be hidden. But if we could see them easily, they would lose their power. If they were right in front of you, anxiously awaiting you to take them, you probably wouldn't take them.

Why?

Because we take for granted what comes easy and what we don't have to work hard for. If everything you ever wanted just showed up in front of you, it wouldn't mean as much to you as if you'd spent time working or looking for these things.

Here's an example. When I visit people who live in lush, green, beautiful areas of the world, I find that they don't have the same appreciation as I do for the beauty around them. I live in the dry, tan landscape of Arizona. The desert has its own beauty, but to be surrounded by green trees and abundant flowers makes my heart soar. When I visit another state, gratitude flows out of me all day as I feast my eyes on the beauty around me, taking it all in—while those who are always in that beauty forget what's right in front of them. I'm sure they have moments of gratitude, but day by day they forget to really enjoy what surrounds them.

This is the benefit of having to find your gifts.

It leaves you in the place of wonder and gratitude when you find them.

One of my favorite books—and a consistent read for me—is *Think and Grow Rich* by Napoleon Hill. I know that seems like a strange reference for this book, but it actually teaches you to how to transform your thoughts into reality. And for me that's worth constantly reading.

In this book, Napoleon talks about his son Blair and the disabilities he was born with, and what Blair chose to do with them. This story alone makes Napoleon's book worth reading.

I'll give you a quick look into Blair's story and how it applies to you.

Blair was born without ears. Literally, his body came into this world without those particular body parts. But that didn't stop him. His father spoke to him every day (placing his lips on the base of his son's head, because this was the most effective way for his son to hear). Napoleon would speak words of belief and ambition to this sweet boy. After years and years of this belief being spoken into his son's mind, Blair grew up to become extremely successful. He was ambitious and had a desire to live a normal life and attain what he wanted from his own hard work.

He came to believe that he could be anything despite his disabilities. When he was in college, he tried many hearing aids, and none worked. Then he chose to test out some experimental hearing aids that had been introduced to him. Napoleon wrote this book in 1937, so hearing-aid technology wasn't very advanced. Blair jumped in and tried these experimental hearing aids and found that full hearing was finally available to him. He then began his life mission, which was to help others with hearing disability.

Are There Really Hidden Gifts Inside This Hell?

As the book states, Blair's purpose was to "render useful service...to bring hope and practical relief to thousands of deafened people who, without his help, would have been doomed forever to deaf mutism."

As I read this story for the second or third time, the thought came to me that maybe this opportunity to serve others was exactly the reason Blair was born with this disability. We could spend all day discussing why Blair was born without ears. Why does anyone have to be deaf?

And of course, the question looms in all our minds: Why does anyone have to endure the madness and pain of sexual abuse?

We have no idea. But those questions are similar to a dog chasing his tail. They spin us around, never getting us anywhere. *Why* questions can keep us stuck. Stuck in anger, and stuck running into walls that never open into doors.

So when we let go of those questions, it leaves us with facts.

And those facts are simple, painful, and real.

One in ten children are sexually abused before they turn eighteen.

These are facts. Chances are, if you're reading this book, you were that one child out of ten.

If there are that many children who are hurting, and as many more adults who are still hurting from their childhood abuse—how do we become like Blair? Where is the hidden gift in this abuse?

It may be hard to even see the word *gifts* next to the words *sexual abuse*. But I invite you to open your mind and heart and begin to look with me as we uncover these gifts.

Somehow this is one of the gifts of being sexually abused. As a survivor of abuse, you can learn to heal and then spread hope through the world to others who are plagued with the pain.

This disability can catapult you forward or be your debilitating sickness.

You get to choose.

The Hidden Gifts

If Blair had been born with ears, he might never have had the gumption and ambition to help solve a problem for deaf people. He might have never become a seeker.

Problems create one of two things: a seeker or a victim.

Seeking is a gift. But you must choose it. And when you do, light will pour down on you, and your own personal gifts and talents will show up.

Every one of us has been born with our own spiritual and physical gifts. But they don't just magically show up. We must be the archaeologists of our life. We must dig and sift and dig some more. The gifts are like finding the bones of a dinosaur. A piece of the gift will show up in an area of our life. But we won't really know what it is, or what that piece belongs to. As we continue to seek and dig, we'll begin to see the whole. The pieces of our gifts will come together to make the final "artifact"—in this case, the full gift.

If you walk through life with the pain of abuse, you're missing the fossils that could be right under your feet. But if you were to grab a shovel and start digging, you might be the lucky one to find the hidden fossil. If you choose to begin the healing process, you'll see that you are the lucky one, uncovering the hidden gifts God has waiting for you, just beyond the reach of seeking.

I know the pain that plagues you. I know the feelings of fear and complacency that permeate your life. And I know you don't want to believe what I'm telling you.

But I promise that if you can set aside the blinders of abuse, grab your shovel, and work with the almighty God, you'll not only uncover your own personal hidden gifts, but you'll find the peace and joy that have been waiting for you.

If you can push through your fears and apprehension with faith, then hope will fill your heart. You may feel as if God has forgotten you. Instead, I believe you're one of His chosen ones, and one of His strongest. You have gifts waiting for you.

Begin your journey, and find them.

Chapter Eleven Journaling

Do you believe that there could be gifts in the hell of abuse? Are you open to looking for them?

The Hidden Gifts

Have you seen any of your spiritual gifts?

Here are a few: feeling others' emotions, hearing what others' needs are, loving others with depth and understanding. Maybe you can discern people and situations with clarity, or you can hear God easily.

There are so many gifts waiting for you to find inside of yourself. I want you to write out ideas of what your spiritual gifts might be.

_____
_____
_____
_____
_____
_____
_____
_____
_____
_____
_____
_____
_____
_____
_____
_____
_____
_____

Are There Really Hidden Gifts Inside This Hell?

The Hidden Gifts

I want you to start a practice of writing down on a piece of paper, or the notepad app on your phone, every time you see a glimmer of a gift. Write down the thoughts and inspiration that comes to your mind. This is how you become the archeologist of your gifts. Start by digging slowly every day; by looking for these gifts and writing down what you see and hear. When you have done this practice for a week or two, journal here what you have found.

_____

_____

_____

_____

_____

_____

_____

_____

_____

_____

_____

_____

_____

_____

_____

_____

_____

_____

Are There Really Hidden Gifts Inside This Hell?

Chapter Twelve
Wash Their Feet

One year prior to my February breakdown, I'd been in the mountains of Arizona. I was at our family cabin with my five kids. God feels much closer for me in those mountains, and this is where I go to seek out answers and guidance.

This particular summer, my main focus and plea to God was how to break the binding pattern of abuse. I'd done enough work with clients to become aware of how emotional patterns continue through the generations.

Sexual abuse is one of the vilest, darkest, and hardest patterns to escape. It's so difficult to escape because of its hidden aspect. Since most people don't speak of abuse that occurred in their family's previous generations, it seems to sneak into our DNA.

No matter what your life looks like, it will find you. It will creep into your life.

I'd seen this, and I begged God to show me how I could heal this generational pattern.

As I was deep in prayer and crying, I was led to a scripture: "And he shall be received by the ordinance of the washing of the feet, for unto this end was the ordinance of washing of feet instituted" (Doctrine and Covenants 88:139).

I was intrigued by this idea of an ordinance of washing feet. I was also confused as to why God would have led me here. So I continued to read on, to verse 141: "He is to gird himself according to the pattern given in the thirteenth chapter of John's testimony."

So, like a treasure hunter, I turned to John chapter 13 in the Bible, searching for the answer.

When I got there, I was taken back by what I was being taught.

Christ knew that He would soon be crucified. He also knew that it would be Judas who would betray Him to the authorities. It was at this time that Christ washed the feet of the apostles. In these verses, Christ is telling his apostles these things: "If I then, your Lord and Master, have washed your feet, ye also ought to wash one another's feet. For I have given you an example, that ye should do as I have done to you. Verily, verily, I say unto you, the servant is not greater than his lord, neither he that is sent greater than he that sent him" (John 13:14-16).

As these verses popped off the page to me, I knew I was to learn from this. But I wasn't quite sure what.

For the next few days, I prayed and thought on these verses and how they could relate to breaking the patterns of abuse.

A few days later, I saw it so clearly.

There were two parts that I was to be learning here.

The first part was realizing what Christ had done. He had known that Judas would betray Him, and yet, He willingly washed all the apostles' feet, including Judas's.

I couldn't comprehend how He did that. How did He, in pure love and service, wash the feet of the very man who not only betrayed Him, but whose actions would ultimately lead Christ to His death?

Then I became aware that this was what Christ was asking *me* to do. I was to wash the feet of my abuser. I was to imagine her there before me, and wash her feet. I was to forgive her and love her, despite what she'd done to me.

I refused. It seemed too much for God to be asking me to do. I could forgive, I could let the abuse go. How could I really imagine washing my abuser's feet?

But my desire to break the pattern of sexual abuse outweighed any other emotion. So I said yes. I would do as God had asked of me.

So I sat there in the middle of the woods one evening when my little ones had gone to sleep. I closed my eyes and imagined washing my abuser's feet. Not only forgiving her, not only having compassion on her, but acting as my Savior had.

I washed her feet.

The experience left me humbled and raw. I felt like I'd just been asked to do one of the hardest things in my life.

But God had more for me to learn.

I saw in my mind's eye that not only was I to wash the feet of my abuser, but I was to wash the feet of my ancestors—those in my generational line who'd been abusers, the ancestors who'd been part of this generational pattern that I'd been sucked in to.

This is where I really refused. I hated those who'd come before me who'd been abusers. I hated those who hadn't stopped the sexual abuse that had gone on for years in the family lines that preceded me.

How could God ask me to do such a thing and wash their feet? *How?* Didn't He know the pain and trauma in every person who'd come from that family line?

My anger at God returned because of the sexual abuse running through so many of my relatives' lives. I was angry that He would even give me the idea to practice this form of forgiveness toward them.

Once again, however, I saw that this was the only way. Because I was so desperate to break this pattern, I set aside my anger and closed my eyes again. There I sat, in the middle of hundreds of trees, the quiet of the forest loud in my ears. I imagined my ancestors who were part of this abuse pattern. One by one, I imagined washing their feet.

This moment is one of deep sacredness to me. One that at first I didn't intend to include in this book. But I can't deny that this is a crucial piece to healing, and one that I must not leave out. So I share this sacred moment with you. As hard as this is to share, I do so in the hope that it will help you as you seek to heal your family line of this black tar. As you seek to cleanse your family of the darkness that has permeated those who came before and those who'll come after you. And even more as you seek to let go of the abuse and the abuser who has had such control of your life. This is the piece that can and will fully release yourself from the madness of abuse.

And yet, this is the first part.

I'm sure you're asking, "How could there even be more?"

As was I.

But then I heard in my heart that there was one more crucial piece. I cry as I write these words, because I know how hard this will be for many of you. I know, because I've heard so many of your stories. And those who've hurt you are among the most evil on earth. The things they've put you through, no person should ever have to endure.

I can't even imagine telling you to do this next part. But I know this is what will heal your heart. This is the piece that will finally detach you from their evil. This is the step that will finally allow you to break free from them and their darkness. But it will be your most painful step.

You must ask God to forgive your abuser for what they did.

I know how impossible this will be for you. It feels impossible because of the absolute hell your abusers caused in your life and in the lives of those who you love. They didn't just mess with your life; they messed with anyone who has been a part of your life. Abuse weaves a chain through every facet of your life, leaving no portion untouched.

So how is it that *you* have to ask God to forgive *them*?

It became clear to me as I screamed at God, "How can you expect me to do this?" I believed that there were some in my family line who deserved to rot and burn in hell for what they'd done. They didn't deserve to be forgiven.

After I'd screamed at God and dug in my heels at this request, in my mind I saw Christ on the cross. I saw Him broken. Broken as I was.

He was bleeding, nailed on the cross, in so much pain. And I heard Him whisper these words: "Father, forgive them, for they know not what they do."

I knew that I'm nothing; I'm not greater than my Savior. And if I'm not greater than He is, then I could do as He did. I could ask God to forgive the girl who'd abused me. I could ask God to forgive those who'd abused the family members who came before me.

God forgive them. Forgive them all.

I was to be the one pleading their case.

As I did so, I felt the breaking of chains—the chains that had bound me to them, and to their darkness, and to their pain.

By asking God to forgive them, I finally released myself from them. Until I had done this, I was bound to them energetically and emotionally. It was the act of pleading for them that finalized the breaking of those binding ties.

It's interesting to sit here on the other side of this experience and see how I was so certain that God had taught me all I needed to learn that summer. I felt so confident that I'd healed and was able to clean up this pattern of abuse.

Little did I know this was only the beginning. God was priming the path for the emotional break that would occur for me eight months later. He was helping me prepare for all that I was to do, one step at a time.

And I actually don't think I'm done. Is there ever a top to this mountain called life?

I believe that there are a series of peaks—there are times when we receive the light, the hope, and the healing, but then there might be a steep cliff that we must go down. The light may seem clouded and darkened as you descend. The lower you go, the darker it gets. Yet miraculously, when you climb up again and reach the next peak, the light grows brighter and more perceptible.

God had taught me these sacred truths in the middle of the woods. But there was more for me to learn and to do. I know without a doubt that I was to write this book. One of my missions is to take the hidden darkness and share it with the world. I know I'm one of the many who must help break the silence and take the secrecy and darkness away from sexual abuse. The only way that's done is by talking, sharing, opening our mouth and speaking truth. My biggest hope and desire is to give light to those who are drowning in the effects of abuse.

As I struggled deeply to write this book, I would sometimes argue with God that I didn't want to do this anymore. I didn't want to always talk about sexual abuse, and I didn't want to hear about the pain and brutality that has occurred for other survivors. The experience of writing kept breaking me again and again. I would continually tell Him that I wasn't strong enough to do this.

On one of those mornings when I'd told God I wouldn't do it any longer, I opened my scriptures, and this is the verse I opened up to:

"And now behold, I, Mormon, do not desire to harrow up the souls of men in casting before them such an awful scene of blood and carnage as was laid before mine eyes, but I, knowing that these things must surely be known, and that all things which are hid must be revealed upon the housetops" (Book of Mormon 5:8).

Once again, I knew that I couldn't run from this. I needed to be one of many voices who could share. It was imperative that I hear the pain that others have gone through so that I would have the motivation to write all these words.

Abuse is like yeast. It grows and flourishes in the dark places. But once a dark secret is brought out of the hidden places and shouted from the rooftops, it can no longer grow. Once light is shed on the dark, the dark dissipates.

We must refuse to keep the abuse a secret. No matter the shame. No matter the hidden pain. We must rise. We must rise as an army of warriors who refuse to let this darkness win any more.

There is power in Christ's light. We must access it to heal ourselves and our generational lines. We are the warriors of light for our families and for ourselves.

No more hiding. No more allowing the darkness to have access to you because of your brokenness.

Take your broken pieces to Christ. Let Him heal you, and then allow Him to teach you what your gifts are. They'll be different from mine. They'll be your own. But they'll be *yours*, and as you use them as directed by Christ through thoughts, impressions, and ideas, you will soar. Every day will be your gift. And you'll be a gift to those around you.

Rise up with me, friend, as a warrior of light. Once you face your hidden pain, it will allow you to rise forth like a phoenix. You'll rise up greater and stronger than ever. Allow the fire of your healing path and Christ's light to heal you and make you into the mighty soul you were created to become.

Chapter Twelve Journaling

How does this concept of "washing the feet of your abuser" feel?

Write out all of your emotions. Do you feel angry, resentful, fearful, bitter, unwillingness to do so?

Wash Their Feet

Before you can actually move forward and visualize washing your abuser's feet, I want you to write for as long as you need to about the anger you feel towards them. Clean all of that out of you. Imagine that writing it all out will be a cleansing agent for your soul.

_____

_____

_____

_____

_____

_____

_____

_____

_____

_____

_____

_____

_____

_____

_____

_____

_____

_____

_____

_____

_____

_____

_____

The Hidden Gifts

Wash Their Feet

After you have written all the pain and anger out, I want you to find a quiet, safe space for you to do the visualization of washing their feet. After you have done this visualization practice, journal your experience. Journal the emotions, the feelings and any ideas or impressions you received at the time.

Wash Their Feet

Now write out your reactions to the idea of asking God to forgive your abuser.

How does it feel to not be asking for God to help **you forgive them,** but instead asking God to *forgive them*? This most likely will be a painful and hard thing to do. I want you to be honest with yourself and write out all the emotions that come up for you around this concept.

The Hidden Gifts

Once you have taken the time to accept this concept, and have chosen to act upon it, write out your experience.

How did it feel to ask God to forgive your abuser? What thoughts, feelings, and impressions did you receive?

_____

_____

_____

_____

_____

_____

_____

_____

_____

_____

_____

_____

_____

_____

_____

_____

_____

_____

_____

The Hidden Gifts

You are a warrior of light. You have been through one of the darkest battles that exist in this world. Yet, you survived. Can you feel that strength deep inside of you? I want you to write about that strength. What do you see, or feel, when you can tap into the strength that is inside of you?

The Hidden Gifts

Chapter Thirteen
"Bring Me Your Suffering..."

As I was in the middle of writing this book, I felt impressed to share with the world my mission—the mission to help find those who are silently suffering, who are filled with deep wounds from sexual abuse. When I found them, I felt impressed to teach them the light that's available from healing these wounds.

As I did that, I had many women reach out and contact me. Each woman had her own individual story of pain.

Each story broke my heart. I felt a deep love and compassion filling me as I had opportunity to see and hear the pain of sexual abuse in many women's lives.

Some stories seemed more horrible than others. But no matter how horrible the abuse was or was not, the pain was the same.

The side-effects were the same.

Suicidal thoughts, depression, anxiety, the need to be perfect or the need to *not* be perfect—all the same.

No matter what the abuse was, these women all felt this pain. These women all ached and struggled the same.

I remember one story in particular. A remarkable woman I'd known for years sent me a message. We'd been acquaintances for a long time, though not close friends. I'd always admired her joyful energy and her vibrant smile.

She reached out to me after one of my Facebook posts about sexual abuse.

Then we had a phone call. And in that phone call, she gave me a brief account of the abuse she'd received.

It was horrific. There's really no word to describe what she went through. I could never have imagined what she told me that day.

My heart was broken after that call. I found myself yelling at God again. This insane rage showed up. I was so angry that God had not saved her from these heinous acts.

Where the hell was He?

My heart broke all day.

I was blown out again.

A question kept coming up: *What the hell was God's plan?* It ruled my day. I wanted to throw myself into every numbing agent possible. I needed to get out of this pain. It wasn't even my pain, yet I'd felt the depth of it, and it was unbearable.

Broken and lost, I went to my worship group that night, hoping to receive the light that illuminates from each of the beautiful women in that group.

As we sat there, I broke down sobbing, begging them to show me how God allows such cruelty and abuse to occur in this world, especially to children.

I told them how I'd spent most of the day begging God to take her story out of my mind. I needed to have it gone. I couldn't exist knowing the type of pain others actually go through.

Then the light came.

They shared with me that this is one tiny speck of the pain Christ felt. One microscopic level of the pain Christ endured.

I was at a loss. I had heard this woman's story and felt just a portion of her pain, and it had left me broken, ready to leave a world where God would allow this.

It was then that I saw an image in my mind. This image was of Christ. His arms were open wide. And He said, "Bring me your suffering."

I wept at the sight of this.

And I realized that I didn't need to know why. But I did know where I could go to receive comfort for my broken heart.

He'd shown me, all those years earlier, in that vision of me broken and bleeding in the pavement of my street corner. He had shown me that when I let Him pick me up, all my wounds were healed.

"Bring me your suffering."

This is where we go. This is where we take our broken pieces and allow Him to heal us.

The pain, the suffering, the inhuman shit that happens—it's all real.

I wish to God that it wasn't. But the more I hear from women reaching out to me with their stories, the more I know how real this is.

And yet I also know how real is the healing power of Christ.

How could He know each one of us? How could He possibly heal all our pain?

This I don't know.

But I've felt His warmth and His light encompass my broken heart. I've felt the heaviness of this pain lifted and eased as I reached out to Him.

Maybe you don't believe in Christ. I'm sure you've experienced anger with God, or you may currently be in that place of rage.

I acknowledge that place. I believe you must go there to fully heal.

I also invite you to plant one tiny seed of faith into your heart. The seed that there might be a Christ, who if you sought Him out, could lift and carry your pain.

Just plant that seed. Let it sit there awhile.

Then take a leap. Start by seeking Christ. Pray to Him. Beg to have your pain taken by Him. Bring Him your suffering and brokenness.

Allow His light to mend your wounds. Receive His healing power that makes you stronger and brighter than you could ever imagine.

Because He is real. I know this as much as I know the sun will rise again every single morning.

He is real.

And He's asking you to bring Him your suffering.

This is your hidden gift.

This opportunity to know Christ, to really know Him, is given to *you*.

You have a chance to seek Him more fully than anyone else.

You have the gift of knowing He is real, more than anyone who has ever needed Him.

When He heals your pain, you'll no longer doubt Him. And moreover, *you will know Him.*

He'll be your friend, and He'll be your Savior in every sense of the word.

The word *Savior* takes on a whole new meaning for those of us who've fallen deep into the pit of pain. The hole that's filled with shame, guilt, haunting memories, fear, rage, insanity. That hole. The one you know all too well. When Christ heals you, He saves you from that hole. He is the ladder out. And not only will He get you out, He will cleanse you and make you whole again. He will save you.

And this is the gift.

This is why I believe we're so special.

It's our pain that leads us to Him. It's our brokenness that brings us to our knees.

Our abuse had made us seekers.

And those who seek will find and be found.

My heart aches more than you know for the tremendous grief and pain you've endured. I write this book for you. I write this book to validate your suffering. I sit here with tears streaming down my face as I think of you. I think of you in your hidden place, with your broken heart. I think of you as you battle your depression and suicidal thoughts and aloneness.

You, my friend, are not alone.

Instead, you belong to a group of some the strongest survivors in this world.

You are a warrior. You're a force to be reckoned with. You'll not be ignored or hidden any longer.

Because I see you. I hear you. And I know you.

And you have so much to offer the world.

You are the gift.

You, my dear friend, are the hidden gift.

Chapter Thirteen Journaling

I want you to write all that is present for you, right now. What thoughts and emotions showed up for you as you read this last chapter?

"Bring Me Your Suffering..."

The Hidden Gifts

Now that you have spent the last 12 chapters addressing the pain and effects of abuse throughout your past and present life, I want you to write out your hope for the future. What would life look like without the pain of your abuse? How would your relationships feel? What would be your most common emotions? I want you to imagine a life that has been cleansed of the pain and the dark effects of abuse. And yet, a life that is strengthened, enriched and rooted deeply because of the healing you have been through. Describe it in as much detail as you can. Be generous and let yourself really dream of what life would feel like.

_____

_____

_____

_____

_____

_____

_____

_____

_____

_____

_____

_____

_____

_____

_____

_____

"Bring Me Your Suffering..."

The Hidden Gifts

"Bring Me Your Suffering..."

Now that you've written this image of your future out, I want you to go back to it regularly. Let yourself feel the peace that is available to you in that image. Really allow yourself to feel the freedom and light that comes from living a life that is not dictated by the abuse. Give yourself permission to hope for this life. I want you to know that hope is your paddle out of the dark. Healing can and will occur as you begin to address the pain that has been hidden for so long. New life shows up when you create from a place of healing and hope. Do you believe that this is possible for you? In this journal space, I want you to write down what time each day you can set aside to sit and meditate on creating this new future. It is also helpful to pick a place in your home where you feel peaceful and safe. Try to meditate in this location every day. It will help create a consistency with your meditation as well as a feeling of safety and comfort.

Time each day:_____

Location in my home:_____

My experience from these "creation meditations:"

_____

_____

_____

_____

_____

_____

_____

_____

The Hidden Gifts

"Bring Me Your Suffering..."

I encourage you to take ten minutes a day to write. Write about anything and everything. Just write. It will be your saving grace and is an excellent form of healing work.

I am so proud of you for taking the time to do these journal entries. These were not easy, and to walk yourself through these journal prompts was courageous and brave. Continue to write. I promise it will be a source of peace for you everyday.

I want you to know that I believe in you. I believe in the light and strength that is in you. I know you and I understand you. Because you are a mirror of me, as I am a mirror of you. You have the strength and the gifts to live life fully and powerfully. Live into those gifts. These gifts will bless your life as well as many people around you.

I send you so much love and support as you walk forward in your healing journey.

{ love and light }

Keira

Preview of the Next Book:
Warriors of Light
Stories of Hope and Healing from Survivors of Sexual Abuse

There's power in uniting. There is light when many combine their voices in truth.

I have a vision of this power blasting through the world, taking out the darkness of sexual abuse. As I finished writing my first book, *The Hidden Gifts Within the Trauma of Sexual Abuse*, I had an idea that hit like a lightning bolt. What if I could compile stories of many survivors of sexual abuse? For any and all who had a story of hope and healing to share, I could give them a platform to share.

This is what this book entails. I can't wait to share with each one of you the power of these survivors. They're true warriors of light. Their stories humbled me, they strengthened me, and they filled me with awe and hope. God bless each one of them for acknowledging their vulnerable stories and for sharing with us the healing that came.

Warrior 1

The brain is such a powerful organ. It seems like so long ago that my abuse happened, but in an instant I can be taken back and remember every detail of what happened and the feelings I had during those five long years.

For the longest time I thought my story of abuse was one of a kind—that I was different, and my story was different, from all the others. I was alone in my abuse.

But as I've grown older and allowed myself to become vulnerable and close to others again, I've found that though we all have our own story, mine isn't all that different from others. My abuser is similar to other people, and my feelings and emotions and the ways the abuse has affected me throughout life are similar to what has been experienced by others. So as I've worked through my past, I've come to know how I'm not alone.

This is a silent suffering with so many people. Though I don't want to shout it from the rooftops, I do want to help others and show the light through healing from the trauma. Because there is light, happiness, and joy in this life. Believe it or not, we can learn and grow from trauma and trials. With that said, it's a battle—and sometimes I still have to force myself to push forward and grab the light. But it becomes easier when we stretch forward.

My abuse started when I was about six years old. I was being babysat by a next-door neighbor after school each day while my parents both worked. The neighbor had three kids of their own right around the ages of my younger sister and me. We became quite close with the family since we were neighbors and went to the same school and got to play every day.

I couldn't tell you the exact day everything changed, when my abuse actually started, but it wasn't long after we started being watched there. Shortly after the abuse began, my dad became very sick with brain cancer, along with my sister having kidney problems. This led my family to spend a lot of time at the hospital.

My care after school would sometimes end with my being rushed to the neighbors while my mom followed the ambulance to the hospital with my dad inside. It was such a scary emotional time in my life. My heart was broken, and I realized this cancer would eventually take my dad's life. I think this is how the abuse got hidden so well, and why I endured it and never said a word. I saw how hard it was on my mom to work and take care of my dad. I saw my dad go from being a strong police officer and my hero to being frail in six years. In my young head I felt it was my job as the oldest to protect my family the best I could, so I endured the pain of abuse because I told myself I was strong, and I shouldn't put another burden on my family.

I remember in school that they would gather all the kids in our grade and have the firefighters and police officers come talk about "stranger danger" or fire safety, and then they would talk about "good touch" and "bad touch." Every time they spoke of bad touch, they would describe an adult as being the bad person. Everything in my being would yell out inside: "That's what has happened to me!" But then I would downplay it, because it wasn't an adult who abused me. It was a friend, a friend my age. Then the guilt and grossness would consume me, and I would wonder: *I must be a bad person because I don't fit the mold of what they're saying.*

It was a constant tug-of-war. I knew I didn't like what was being done to me, and I begged for it to stop. Every time I would try to rebel against it, I would get threats of being in trouble, or that lies would be said about me. I feared my parents finding out, and I feared the disappointment that would go with it and the burden they would bear. I feared it would make life harder on them.

One time I did rebel and refused to let the abuse happen. And just as the person had threatened, a lie was told and I got in trouble at the babysitter's. While I sat in time-out for what seemed like a really long time, the kids would come and make fun of me. It was embarrassing and it humiliated me. I remember crying and realizing I had no power, and I wondered when this part of my life would pass.

About five years later, I felt I was old enough to stay home after school and take care of my sister and myself. I convinced my mom that I was strong enough to do it, and I mentioned if I had any trouble, the neighbors were right down the street and we would have help if we needed it. I promised to call her at work every day after school, and to not use the stove or sharp knives, and that everything would be okay.

After begging her time and again, she agreed. I knew this was my out. The abuse would finally stop. From that point, it did. I hung out with the neighbor kids much less often, and when I did, I knew I had an out. Life seemed great again. I had some much needed peace.

Well, at least the anxiety from the abuse stopped, but the feelings of guilt and dirtiness lingered. How does someone allow such dirty things to happen to them? To survive these feelings, I would push them deep down inside. I had to, because it would consume me. And to be honest, I was fighting the battle, knowing my dad wouldn't live much longer.

A little less than two years later, he passed away. The grief was so great that my focus wasn't on the pain of my abuse but the pain of losing my dad.

But the pain of abuse rears its ugly head time and time again, and for me it continued to do so throughout my growing up. It affected my relationships with everyone I came in contact with. I would never allow others to get close to me. It affected my happiness in life. Nothing really had any pure joy or excitement behind it. I was closed off because I'd been hurt so much that I didn't trust anyone, and my self-esteem was on the floor. I had nothing to offer anyone because I wasn't a good person because of my past. It was a heavy burden to bear and a lonely place to be in.

Then one day I met the man of my dreams. I was able to love him and learned to trust him. We were married young and started having children young. For quite a few years I never told him of my abuse. I thought that would be something that would make him pull away. But I saw the abuse affecting my marriage. I still didn't let him come too close emotionally. I always feared the day would come when he realized he was better than me, and would leave, because I wasn't enough.

He stuck by my side, and eventually, one day, I told him of all the pain I'd been holding on to. To my surprise, he didn't run. He didn't even bat an eye. He hugged me and loved me. He listened and told me it wasn't my fault. He was my rock. So for years he was the only one who knew. And in that moment, I loved him even more.

Telling him did bring some relief from the pain, but my thoughts continued to be a battle in my head no matter how hard I tried to tell myself it wasn't my fault.

About eight years later, I'd just had my fourth daughter and moved into a beautiful home that my husband had built. Life seemed like it really couldn't get any better. I felt that for the most part I'd overcome the thoughts in my head, until my third daughter died in an unexpected accident. It was the most horrific day of my life. Everything in my life came crashing down around me. There isn't any amount of words to describe the pain of losing my sweet daughter.

In that moment I was broken, the most broken I'd ever felt. I convinced myself that she was gone because of me. I wasn't a good mother, and I wasn't a good mother because of the person I was. I was a lie because of my past.

But then, as always, there was a glimmer of who I truly knew I was. I was a child of God, I had a pure heart, and there was a small amount of me that knew the abuse wasn't my fault and that it was something that was done to me. I was good.

But having my daughter die broke me to the core, and everything I believed in was truly put to the test. Did I really believe I would see her again after death? Did I really believe that we're an eternal family? Does my heavenly Father care about us and truly love us? And if He does, does He allow bad things to happen? Or why doesn't He rescue us from this heartache and pain? Why didn't He save her? Did I believe all these things I'd been taught all my life and things that I'd built a testimony on, and testified of? Here I was, with a heart shattered and completely broken.

It wasn't until we went to the funeral home to dress my daughter for the funeral on the following day that things really changed for me. I was blessed to go with my family and dress my beautiful daughter and hold her for one last time on this earth. It was probably one of the most spiritual experiences I've ever had in my life.

We then decided as a family what we should do after. My father-in-law suggested going to the visitors center at the temple. Mark Mabry had just displayed all the pictures he'd done on Christ's life. (If you haven't seen these pictures, they're a must! Absolutely the most beautifully done pictures of Christ's life, and the collection is called "The Reflections of Christ.") We agreed and walked the temple grounds, and then entered the visitors center. There was a beautiful peace that overcame me. It's like time stood still for me as I viewed each picture. Each one encompassed me as I put myself in those pictures.

I then walked up to the picture of Christ on the cross. The most incredible emotions came over me. I began to cry, and my tears were tears of sadness, but also of love and joy. In that moment I felt my heavenly Father and Christ's love for me as I've never felt before. I had a love for them I'd never experienced before. I felt understood, and I felt like I understood them.

We shared something in common at the point. I had a glimpse of the pain my heavenly Father felt when Christ died. I also felt an overcoming love for Christ because this picture represented His suffering for me. He suffered and died for me, and for all the suffering and pains I'd felt. I realized in this moment it wasn't just for my sins, but for everything I went through in this life. He felt it all, every little bit of it. He knew me, He loved me, He hurt for me.

In that moment, the healing in my life began. I reached out and got help. I went to a counselor and thought it would be only to work through the death of my daughter. But I also got the courage to work through the pain of being molested. I was able to forgive the friend who hurt me, and I realized that for her to do what she did to me at such a young age, it had to have been done to her. She had to be a victim, because young children are innocent, and she wouldn't have known all she did had it not been done to her. I forgave her and began working on forgiving myself.

With all this healing, the sun in my life shone brighter than it ever had. This didn't all happen overnight. It was scary and a struggle for years. I fell into a depression after my daughter's death. I didn't want to live and wanted to disappear from this earth. But all along, I felt my heavenly Father's hand leading and guiding me to get the help I needed, and when the darkness would lift, the light was incredible.

Now, almost ten years later, my joy and happiness are more than I could have imagined. Do I still have dark moments from time to time? Yes, but it's the in-between that's awesome! I've learned and grown more than I ever thought I could. I love more deeply than I ever thought I could. I still worry it could all be taken away, but I now know how to work through that. I am strong, and I have a more fulfilled life.

None of us leave this life without experiencing the darkness, but we are light. We're born with the light of Christ. We aren't alone, and it's in those moments that He carries us. And if we'll let Him, He will love and teach us through our darkest experiences. Then we can be a light to others. We are strong, and this is the plan of happiness, if we truly work to seek it.

If you have a story of hope and healing that you would love to share with others who experience the darkness that comes from sexual abuse, email me. I would love to share your story in my upcoming book, *Warriors of Light*. My hope is that this next book will bring more light to those who are struggling with the effects of sexual abuse, as well as give survivors a platform to share their stories of hope and healing. There is strength that comes from sharing. There is peace that comes from knowing that you are not alone. I would love to help you bring your story into the world and allow it help those who need to hear it. These stories can be shared with your name, or anonymously. You can email me at *contact@keirapoulsen.com*.

And if you would like to follow me along on any of my social media accounts, this is where you can find me:

Instagram: *@keirapoulsen   @projectbreakthesilence*

Facebook: *@createyourself.keirapoulsen*

Website: *www.keirapoulsen.com*

Acknowledgments

I want to thank God for this book. I had spent two weeks in the fall of 2017 with a constant "nagging" feeling that I needed to write a book. I began to pray and ask for guidance around what topic I would need to write. Soon after I had been asking God to show me the book I would need to write, I received an answer that ultimately altered the course of my life.

I was driving home one evening and out of nowhere I saw an image flash in my mind's eye. The image I saw was a book. I viewed this book from the top down, and it currently appears exactly how I had seen it, with this exact title in bold letters. "The Hidden Gifts Within the Trauma of Sexual Abuse." I had never thought of these words together in my life, nor had I planned on writing a book about healing from sexual abuse. Yet, here it was. I felt like I had been punched in the gut when I read this title in my mind. Tears began to flow from my eyes, and I cannot deny that God had sent this book title to me. I was so scared to write this book and felt very overwhelmed at the idea of even attempting to. When I finally agreed that this was the book I was to write, I was surprised to see how the words began to come with ease. I would be awakened at 4:00 am many days with chapters flowing out of my hands. It was a sacred experience and one that truly has changed me as a person.

I am thankful to my husband, Dan. He believed in me from the beginning. He never doubted me or this work and has supported me in every way possible as I have created this book. I want to thank my five beautiful children, Kale, Eli, Beck, Presley and Jones, for always believing in me.

Acknowledgments

They are my biggest supporters and cheerleaders! I am so grateful for their love.

I am thankful for my parents, Steven and Joyce Brinton. It is their love of self-transformation and emotional work that has shaped me into the person that I am. I am grateful for the pieces that they have been on this path for me, and the support they have given me. Their wisdom and their gifts have been crucial in my own personal development and the healing work that I currently do.

I am thankful for my siblings Loren, Claire and Hannah for always loving me, and being my best friends. They helped me push forward with so many aspects of my book. Thank you!!

I am forever grateful for my therapist, guru, angel, Glenda Horning. She was a light to me when I was drowning in the dark. Her work of Rapid Eye Therapy broke years and years of pain and darkness for me. It was in her office that I felt the healing power of Christ so powerfully that it felt tangible to the touch. Thank you, Glenda, for your love, wisdom and your beautiful gifts.

I am thankful for my wonderful editor Thomas Womak. He took a chance with me and this sacred project. Thomas was able to clean up my words and bring clarity to the ideas that were running through my mind. He did such a wonderful job.

I am thankful for my artist, Marie Lee. She was able to listen to my ideas for the artwork and then created them to fit the images that were in my mind. She is so gifted, and I am so grateful for her lovely artwork that is throughout this book. I am grateful for Katie Mullaly at Surrogate Press for her beautiful formatting of this book! She was able to take all of my writing, artwork, and journaling pages and compiled it beautifully. Thank you! I am also thankful for my sister in law Lara Stowell for editing the journal pages and helping me when I was in need.

I am grateful to the beautiful souls in my worship group. They were such a support to me when I would struggle with the fears that came up for me while writing this book. Their love and their support pulled me through my heaviest days. I love each one of them for their presence in my life. You are my soul sisters in so many ways.

I want to thank each and every survivor of sexual abuse who reached out to me during this time. Your story matters to me, more than you know. Your pain and your experience gave me the strength to keep writing even when the darkness seemed to want to put my own light out. You are the warriors who inspire me to stand up and share.

I give God the glory in the writing of this book and also in the life that I live. I am grateful to have been blessed to author this book and to be a voice for those who need a voice. I consider it an honor and privilege to be one of many people who are breaking the silence on sexual abuse and bringing the dark into the light.

About the Author

Keira Poulsen is a mother of five children. She and her husband currently live in Arizona. Keira has a deep love for self-transformational work and healing. Keira is a life coach for women. She is trained in Energy Mastery work as well as Muscle Testing. She uses these tools along with many other tools to help the women that she coaches.

Keira is a public speaker. She speaks to groups of women on subjects of creating your life, finding the hidden gifts within trauma, and the purpose of pain.

Keira has recently started a publishing company, Freedom House Publishing Co. This company is dedicated solely to helping women write their stories of hope and healing and giving them the freedom to share these stories with the world.

Most of all, Keira is passionate about bringing light to the topics that most people are afraid to address. She loves to spread the message of hope into the topics that are stifled with fear. There are many programs, and courses she is creating that will be available in the near future to help those who want freedom from their past, and to learn how to create their futures.

Index

Page 1: "Then Peter opened his mouth, and said, Of a truth I perceive that God is no respecter or persons." Acts 10:34.

Page 10: "We cannot learn without pain." Aristotle.

Page 11: "The wound is where the light enters you." Persian Poet Rumi.

Page 11: "The cure for the pain is the pain." Persian Poet Rumi.

Page 16: "There is no such thing as a problem without a gift for you in its hands." Richard Bach from the book *Illusions: the Adventures of a Reluctant Messiah*.

Page 36: "oh God…" D&C 121: 1-2.

Page 36: "My son…" D&C 121:7-8.

Page 85: "Ask, and it shall be given you; seek, and ye shall find; knock, and it shall be opened unto you: for every one that asketh receiveth; and he that seeketh findeth; and to him that knocketh it shall be opened." Matthew 7:7-8.

Page 100: "You can't go back and make a new start, but you can start right now and make a brand new ending." James R. Sherman from the book *Rejection*.

Page 101: "We can complain that rose bushes have thorns or rejoice because thorn bushes have roses." Abraham Lincoln.

Index

Page 134: *Think and Grow Rich* by Napoleon Hill.

Page 135: Statistic for 1 out f 10 children are sexually abused. David Finkelhor, Anne Shattuck, Heather A. Turner, & Sherry L. Hamby, "The Lifetime Prevalence of Child Sexual Abuse and Sexual Assault Assessed in Late Adolescence," 55 *Journal of Adolescent Health,* 329, 329-333 (2014).

Page 143: "And he shall be received by the ordinance of the washing of the feet, for unto this end was the ordinance of the washing of feet instituted." D&C 88:139.

Page 143: "He is to gird himself according to the pattern given in the thirteenth chapter of John's testimony." D&C 88:141.

Page 143: "If I then, your Lord and Master, have washed your feet, ye also ought to wash one another's feet. For I have given you an example, that ye should do as I have done to you. Verily, verily, I say unto you, the servant is not greater than his lord, neither he that is sent greater than he that sent him." John 13:14-16.

Page 146: "Father, forgive them, for they know not what they do." Luke 23:34.

Page 147: "And now behold, I, Mormon, do not desire to harrow up the souls of men in casting before them such an awful scene of blood and carnage as was laid before mine eyes, but I, knowing that these things must surely be known, and that all things which are hid must be revealed upon the house-tops." Book of Mormon 5:8.

Made in the USA
San Bernardino, CA
17 January 2019